As I Walked Out One Evening

As I Walked Out One Evening

Songs, Ballads, Lullabies, Limericks, and Other Light Verse

by W. H. Auden

821
A899

SELECTED BY EDWARD MENDELSON

Vintage International
Vintage Books
A Division of Random House, Inc.
New York

HUMCA

A VINTAGE INTERNATIONAL ORIGINAL, AUGUST 1995
First edition

Library of Congress Cataloging-in-Publication Data
Auden, W. H. (Wystan Hugh), 1907–1973.
As I walked out one evening : songs, ballads, lullabies,
limericks, and other light verse / W. H. Auden ; selected by Edward Mendelson.
—Vintage International original 1st ed.
p.   cm.
Includes index.
ISBN 0-679-76170-5
1. Humorous poetry, English.   I. Mendelson, Edward.   II. Title.
PR6001.U4A6   1995
811'.52—dc20   95-5428
CIP

Book design by Rebecca Aidlin

Contents

Preface ix

It's No Use Raising a Shout   3
What's in Your Mind, My Dove, My Coney   5
Prothalamion   6
Alma Mater   8
The Airman's Alphabet   10
The Three Companions   13
Shorts   14
Song: You were a great Cunarder, I   18
Ballad: O what is that sound which so thrills the ear   19
The Witnesses   21
Song: Seen when night was silent   27
Who's Who   28
Now Through Night's Caressing Grip   29
In the Square   30
Madrigal   32
Night Mail   33
Song: Let the florid music praise   36
Foxtrot from a Play   37
Underneath the Abject Willow   39
Fish in the Unruffled Lakes   40
Song: The chimney sweepers   41
At Last the Secret Is Out   42
Funeral Blues   43
Jam Tart   44
Death's Echo   45
Letter to Lord Byron   47
Lullaby: Lay your sleeping head, my love   86

Danse Macabre 88

Blues: Ladies and gentlemen, sitting here 91

Give Up Love 92

Nonsense Song 94

Johnny 95

Miss Gee 96

Victor 100

James Honeyman 105

Roman Wall Blues 110

As I Walked Out One Evening 111

O Tell Me the Truth About Love 113

Gare du Midi 115

Epitaph on a Tyrant 116

The Unknown Citizen 117

Refugee Blues 118

Ode 120

Calypso 122

Heavy Date 123

Song: Warm are the still and lucky miles 128

"Gold in the North" Came the Blizzard to Say 129

The Glamour Boys and Girls Have Grievances Too 130

Carry Her Over the Water 132

Eyes Look into the Well 133

Lady Weeping at the Crossroads 134

Notes 136

The Way 141

Song for St Cecilia's Day 142

Many Happy Returns 145

Shepherd's Carol 149

Song of the Old Soldier 151

Song of the Master and Boatswain 152

Adrian and Francisco's Song 153

Miranda's Song 154

Three Songs from *The Age of Anxiety*   155
Under Which Lyre   157
Nursery Rhyme   163
Barcarolle   164
Music Ho   165
The Love Feast   166
Song: Deftly, admiral, cast your fly   167
Limericks   168
Hunting Season   170
The Willow-Wren and the Stare   171
The Proof   173
"The Truest Poetry Is the Most Feigning"   174
Nocturne   177
Metalogue to *The Magic Flute*   178
A Toast   182
Some Thirty Inches from My Nose   184
On the Circuit   185
Song of the Ogres   188
Song of the Devil   189
The Geography of the House   191
Moralities   194
A New Year Greeting   201
Doggerel by a Senior Citizen   203

Notes   207

Index of Titles and First Lines   215

Preface

This book is a selection of Auden's most immediately accessible poems. These poems, which include some of his greatest work, have all the profundity and complexity of his more difficult poems, but they also have the direct emotional and rhythmic appeal of traditional ballads, popular songs, rhyming games for children, and rude limericks for adults. In writing each of these poems, Auden challenged himself to transform a conventional form or familiar style into a fresh source of wisdom, surprise, and delight. And he chose to write many of his poems in accessible styles because they allowed him to write about emotions and experiences that more difficult and obscure styles would falsify or distort.

Unlike many of his contemporary poets, Auden did not write in one manner for an elite learned audience and another style for a larger popular audience. In fact, he did not write for any collective or general audience at all. He wrote for each of his individual readers, and for each of the variations and moods in each reader's life. He knew that a reader who in one mood prefers tragedy will want farce in another, and that the most serious moods do not necessarily call for the most solemn poems:

> Even a limerick
> ought to be something a man of
> honor, awaiting death from cancer or a firing-squad,
> could read without contempt: (at
> *that* frontier I wouldn't dare speak to anyone
> in either a prophet's bellow
> or a diplomat's whisper.)

He wrote these lines late in his life, in "The Cave of Making," an elegy for his fellow poet Louis MacNeice. Three decades earlier, in "Letter to Lord Byron," he had written in a similar vein:

Only on varied diet can we live.
The pious fable and the dirty story
Share in the total literary glory.

Auden's first published book, *Poems,* appeared in 1930, when he was twenty-three. His friend Naomi Mitchison complained in a review that some of the poems were overly obscure. "Am I really so obscure?" he asked her in a letter. "Obscurity is a bad fault." He was then emerging from a phase in which he had tried to outdo the early T. S. Eliot in writing poems made up of fragments and allusions, and he had begun to write verse that he hoped would be as suitable for the cabaret and theater as for the printed page.

From 1932 through 1938 he wrote musical plays for the experimental and often chaotic productions of a London-based company called the Group Theatre. The Group (which had no connection with the New York company of the same name) was the creation of the dancer Rupert Doone and the painter Robert Medley; it had been Medley who started Auden on his career as a poet by casually asking him at school if he had ever written any poems. Auden wrote almost all his work for the Group in collaboration—his plays were written jointly with Christopher Isherwood, with lyrics written to be set by Benjamin Britten—and the shared act of collaboration helped him escape the solitary obscurities of his earliest poems. At the same time, he found that he could write most easily about his emotional life in songs for the soprano voice of Hedli Anderson (whom he met when she performed with the Group Theatre). Behind the mask of Hedli Anderson he could tell truths that would sound egocentric and false if he spoke them in his own person.

For a few years after he settled in America in 1939, he continued to write song lyrics, some of them in calypso and Wild West accents that he had not heard in England. But during the 1940s and 1950s, his songs became more contemplative and infrequent, and instead of musical plays he wrote opera libretti in collaboration with Chester Kallman. In the 1960s, however, he again began writing lighter poems for public performance. The initial impulse was a commission to write the lyrics for the musical comedy *Man of La Mancha,* although the producer found Auden's contributions too thoughtful and replaced him with a lyricist more palatable for Broadway. Also in the 1960s, his agent began to arrange annual reading tours for him at American colleges and universities, and many of his later poems were written to unsettle and delight the listeners who, with a generosity that always amazed him, paid to hear him read. He also read to poetry festivals and other audiences in America and Europe, and died a few hours after his last public reading, in Vienna in 1973.

The poems in this book have been chosen according to the principles that Auden specified in his introduction to *The Oxford Book of Light Verse,* an anthology that he compiled in 1937:

> When the things in which the poet is interested, the things which he sees about him, are much the same as those of his audience, and that audience is a fairly general one, he will not be conscious of himself as an unusual person, and his language will be straightforward and close to ordinary speech. When, on the other hand, his interests and perceptions are not readily acceptable to society, or his audience is a highly specialized one, perhaps of fellow poets, he will be acutely aware of himself as the poet, and his method of expression may depart very widely from the normal social language.
>
> In the first case his poetry will be "light" in the sense in which it is used in this anthology. Three kinds of poetry have been included:
>
> 1. Poetry written for performance, to be spoken or sung before an audience (e.g., Folk-songs, the poems of Tom Moore).
>
> 2. Poetry intended to be read, but having for its subject-matter the everyday social life of its period or the experiences of the poet as an ordinary human being (e.g., the poems of Chaucer, Pope, Byron).
>
> 3. Such nonsense poetry as, through its properties and techniques, has a general appeal (Nursery rhymes, the poems of Edward Lear).

Auden recognized this kind of poetry as a distinct category in his own work. He used the title "Lighter Poems" for one of the sections of *Another Time,* a book of poems that he published in 1940. In the collected edition of his work that he published in 1945, he gathered many of his lighter poems under the heading "Songs and Other Musical Pieces"; in a collected edition published in 1966, he gathered them in groups titled "Ten Songs," "Twelve Songs," and similar headings.

The arrangement of this book is chronological. A few poems are included that Auden never published or that he published in magazines but never collected in book form.

Edward Mendelson

As I Walked Out One Evening

It's No Use Raising a Shout

It's no use raising a shout.
No, Honey, you can cut that right out.
I don't want any more hugs;
Make me some fresh tea, fetch me some rugs.
Here am I, here are you:
But what does it mean? What are we going to do?

A long time ago I told my mother
I was leaving home to find another:
I never answered her letter
But I never found a better.
Here am I, here are you:
But what does it mean? What are we going to do?

It wasn't always like this?
Perhaps it wasn't, but it is.
Put the car away; when life fails,
What's the good of going to Wales?
Here am I, here are you:
But what does it mean? What are we going to do?

In my spine there was a base,
And I knew the general's face:
But they've severed all the wires,
And I can't tell what the general desires.
Here am I, here are you:
But what does it mean? What are we going to do?

In my veins there is a wish,
And a memory of fish:
When I lie crying on the floor,
It says, "You've often done this before."
Here am I, here are you:
But what does it mean? What are we going to do?

A bird used to visit this shore:
It isn't going to come any more.
I've come a very long way to prove
No land, no water, and no love.
Here am I, here are you:
But what does it mean? What are we going to do?

What's in Your Mind, My Dove, My Coney

What's in your mind, my dove, my coney;
Do thoughts grow like feathers, the dead end of life;
Is it making of love or counting of money,
Or raid on the jewels, the plans of a thief?

Open your eyes, my dearest dallier;
Let hunt with your hands for escaping me;
Go through the motions of exploring the familiar;
Stand on the brink of the warm white day.

Rise with the wind, my great big serpent;
Silence the birds and darken the air;
Change me with terror, alive in a moment;
Strike for the heart and have me there.

Prothalamion

You who return to-night to a narrow bed
With one name running sorrowfully through your sorrowful head,
You who have never been touched, and you, pale lover,
Who left the house this morning kissed all over,
You little boys also of quite fourteen
Beginning to realise just what we mean,
Fill up glasses with champagne and drink again.

It's not a new school or factory to which we summon,
We're here today because of a man and a woman.
O Chef, employ your continental arts
To celebrate the union of two loving hearts.
Waiters, be deft, and slip, you pages, by
To honour the god to name whom is to lie:
Fill up glasses with champagne and drink again.

Already he has brought the swallows past the Scillies
To chase each other skimming under English bridges,
Has loosed the urgent pollen on the glittering country
To find the pistil, force its burglar's entry,
He moves us also and up the marble stair
He leads the figures matched in beauty and desire:
Fill up glasses with champagne and drink again.

It's not only this we praise, it's the general love:
Let cat's mew rise to a scream on the tool-shed roof,
Let son come home to-night to his anxious mother,
Let the vicar lead the choirboy into a dark corner.
The orchid shall flower to-night that flowers every hundred years,
The boots and the slavey be found dutch-kissing on the stairs:
Fill up glasses with champagne and drink again.

Let this be kept as a generous hour by all,
This once let the uncle settle his nephew's bill,
Let the nervous lady's table gaucheness be forgiven,
Let the thief's explanation of the theft be taken,
The boy caught smoking shall escape the usual whipping,
To-night the expensive whore shall give herself for nothing:
Fill up glasses with champagne and drink again.

The landlocked state shall get its port to-day,
The midnight worker in the laboratory by the sea
Shall discover under the cross-wires that which he looks for,
To-night the asthmatic clerk shall dream he's a boxer,
Let the cold heart's wish be granted, the desire for a desire,
O give to the coward now his hour of power:
Fill up glasses with champagne and drink again.

Alma Mater

Chorus.   Hail the strange electric writing
                Alma Mater on the door
                Like a secret sign inviting
                All the rich to meet the poor:
                Alma Mater, ave, salve,
                Floreas in secula.

Girls.   You sent us men with lots of money,
                You sent us men you knew were clean,
                You sent us men as sweet as honey,
                Men to make us really keen.
                Always, even though we marry,
                Though we wear ancestral pearls,
                One memory we'll always carry,
                We were Alma Mater girls.

Chorus.   Alma Mater, ave, salve, *etc.*

Thieves.   Let Americans with purses
                Go for short strolls after dark,
                Let the absent-minded nurses
                Leave an heiress in the park,
                Though the bullers soon or later
                Clap us handcuffed into jail,
                We'll remember Alma Mater,
                We'll remember without fail.

Chorus.   Alma Mater, ave, salve, *etc.*

Boys.   The French are mean and Germans lazy,
                Dutchmen leave you in the end.
                Only the English, though they're crazy,
                They will keep you for a friend.
                Always, though a king in cotton

Waft us hence to foreign parts,
Alma Mater shall not be forgotten,
She is written on our hearts.

Chorus.   Alma Mater, ave, salve, *etc.*

Blackmailers.   We must thank our mugs' relations,
For our income and man's laws.
But the first congratulations,
Alma Mater, they are yours.

Coiners.   When the fool believes our story,
When he thinks our coins are true,
To Alma Mater be the glory
For she taught us what to do.

Chorus.   Alma Mater, ave, salve, *etc.*

Old Hacks   We cannot dance upon the table
and Trots.   Now we're old as souvenirs
Yet as long as we are able
We'll remember bygone years.
Still, as when we were the attraction,
Come the people from abroad,
Spending, though we're out of action,
More than they can well afford.

Chorus.   Alma Mater, ave, salve, *etc.*

Grand Chorus.   Navies rust and nations perish,
Currency is never sure,
But Alma Mater she shall flourish
While the sexes shall endure:
Alma Mater, ave, salve,
Floreas in secula.

The Airman's Alphabet

ACE—
Pride of parents
and photographed person
and laughter in leather.

BOMB—
Curse from cloud
and coming to crook
and saddest to steeple.

COCKPIT—
Soft seat
and support of soldier
and hold for hero.

DEATH—
Award for wildness
and worst in the west
and painful to pilots.

ENGINE—
Darling of designers
and dirty dragon
and revolving roarer.

FLYING—
Habit of hawks
and unholy hunting
and ghostly journey.

GAUGE—
Informer about oil
and important to eye
and graduated glass.

HANGAR—
Mansion of machine
and motherly to metal
and house of handshaking.

INSTRUMENT—
Dial on dashboard
and destroyer of doubt
and father of fact.

JOYSTICK—   Pivot of power
             and responder to pressure
             and grip for the glove.

KISS—   Touch taking off
             and tenderness in time
             and firmness on flesh.

LOOPING—   Flying folly
             and feat at fairs
             and brave to boys.

MECHANIC—   Owner of overalls
             and interested in iron
             and trusted with tools.

NOSE-DIVE—   Nightmare to nerves
             and needed by no one
             and dash toward death.

OBSERVER—   Peeper through periscope
             and peerer at pasture
             and eye in the air.

PROPELLER—   Wooden wind-oar
             and twisted whirler
             and lifter of load.

QUIET—   Absent from airmen
             and easy to horses
             and got in the grave.

RUDDER—   Deflector of flight
             and flexible fin
             and pointer of path.

STORM—   Night from the north
             and numbness nearing
             and hail ahead.

TIME—   Expression of alarm
                        and used by the ill
                        and personal space.

UNDERCARRIAGE—   Softener of shock
                        and seat on the soil
                        and easy to injure.

VICTIM—   Corpse after crash
                        and carried through country
                        and atonement for aircraft.

WIRELESS—   Sender of signal
                        and speaker of sorrow
                        and news from nowhere.

X—   Mark upon map
                        and meaning mischief
                        and lovers' lingo.

YOUTH—   Daydream of devils
                        and dear to the damned
                        and always to us.

ZERO—   Love before leaving
                        and touch of terror
                        and time of attack.

The Three Companions

"O where are you going?" said reader to rider,
"That valley is fatal where furnaces burn,
　Yonder's the midden whose odours will madden,
　That gap is the grave where the tall return."

"O do you imagine", said fearer to farer,
"That dusk will delay on your path to the pass,
　Your diligent looking discover the lacking
　Your footsteps feel from granite to grass?"

"O what was that bird", said horror to hearer,
"Did you see that shape in the twisted trees?
　Behind you swiftly the figure comes softly,
　The spot on your skin is a shocking disease?"

"Out of this house"—said rider to reader
"Yours never will"—said farer to fearer
"They're looking for you"—said hearer to horror
　As he left them there, as he left them there.

Shorts

Pick a quarrel, go to war
Leave the hero in the bar.
Hunt the lion, climb the peak.
No one guesses you are weak.

. . .

The friends of the born nurse
Are always getting worse.

. . .

You're a long way off from becoming a saint
As long as you suffer from any complaint:
But if you don't, there's no denying
The chances are that you're not trying.

. . .

Man would be happy, loving and sage
If he didn't keep lying about his age.

. . .

Tommy did as mother told him
    Till his soul had split:
One half thought of angels
    And the other half of shit.

. . .

Willy, finding half a soul,
Went abroad to find the whole.
He went by land, he went by sea
But never found it: Thomas Cook
For every effort that he took
Received the customary fee.

.　.　.

Desire for death in the morning
　　　Is cancer's warning.
Desire for life at night
　　　Is mania in sight.

.　.　.

Schoolboy, making lonely maps:
Better do it with some chaps.

.　.　.

The pleasures of the English nation:
Copotomy and Sodulation.

.　.　.

Let us honour if we can
The vertical man
Though we value none
But the horizontal one.

.　.　.

I am beginning to lose patience
With my personal relations.
They are not deep
And they are not cheap.

. . .

I'm afraid there's many a spectacled sod
Prefers the British Museum to God.

. . .

There are two kinds of friendship even in babes:
Two against one and seven against Thebes.

. . .

Private faces in public places
Are wiser and nicer
Than public faces in private places.

. . .

Come kiss me now, you old brown cow
The doctor's said you're balmy.
The maid at the vicar's has torn her knickers
I'm off to join the army.

. . .

Don't know my father's name,
I am my mother's shame.
I mayn't die all the same,
   I'm still too young.

     . . .

If yer wants to see me agyne
   Then come to the stytion before the tryne.
In the general wytin' 'all
   We'll see each other fer the very las' time of all.

     . . .

Alice is gone and I'm alone,
   Nobody understands
How lovely were her Fire Alarms,
   How fair her German Bands.

O how I cried when Alice died
   The day we were to have wed.
We never had our Roasted Duck
   And now she's a Loaf of Bread.

At nights I weep, I cannot sleep:
   Moonlight to me recalls
I never saw her Waterfront
   Nor she my Waterfalls.

Song

You were a great Cunarder, I
Was only a fishing smack.
Once you passed across my bows
And of course you did not look back.
It was only a single moment yet
I watch the sea and sigh,
Because my heart can never forget
The day you passed me by.

Ballad

O what is that sound which so thrills the ear
  Down in the valley drumming, drumming?
Only the scarlet soldiers, dear,
  The soldiers coming.

O what is that light I see flashing so clear
  Over the distance brightly, brightly?
Only the sun on their weapons, dear,
  As they step lightly.

O what are they doing with all that gear;
  What are they doing this morning, this morning?
Only the usual manœuvres, dear,
  Or perhaps a warning.

O why have they left the road down there;
  Why are they suddenly wheeling, wheeling?
Perhaps a change in the orders, dear;
  Why are you kneeling?

O haven't they stopped for the doctor's care;
  Haven't they reined their horses, their horses?
Why, they are none of them wounded, dear,
  None of these forces.

O is it the parson they want with white hair;
  Is it the parson, is it, is it?
No, they are passing his gateway, dear,
  Without a visit.

O it must be the farmer who lives so near;
  It must be the farmer so cunning, so cunning?
They have passed the farm already, dear,
  And now they are running.

O where are you going? stay with me here!
    Were the vows you swore me deceiving, deceiving?
No, I promised to love you, dear,
        But I must be leaving.

O it's broken the lock and splintered the door,
    O it's the gate where they're turning, turning;
Their feet are heavy on the floor
        And their eyes are burning.

The Witnesses

I

You dowagers with Roman noses
Sailing along between banks of roses
       well dressed,
You Lords who sit at committee tables
And crack with grooms in riding stables
       your father's jest;

Solicitors with poker faces,
And doctors with black bags to cases
       hurried,
Reporters coming home at dawn
And heavy bishops on the lawn
       by sermons worried;

You stokers lit by furnace-glare,
And you, too, steeplejacks up there
       singing,
You shepherds wind-blown on the ridges,
Tramps leaning over village bridges
       your eardrums ringing;

On land, on sea, in field, in town
Attend: Musician put them down,
       those trumpets;
Let go, young lover, of her hand
Come forward both of you and stand
       as still as limpets

Close as you can and listen well:
My companion here is about to tell
       a story;
Peter, Pontius Pilate, Paul
Whoever you are, it concerns you all
       and human glory.

Call him Prince Alpha if you wish
He was born in a palace, his people were swish;
     his christening
Was called by the Tatler the event of the year,
All the photographed living were there
     and the dead were listening.

You would think I was trying to foozle you
If I told you all that kid could do;
     enough
To say he was never afraid of the dark
He climbed all the trees in his pater's park;
     his nurse thought him rough.

At school his brilliance was a mystery,
All languages, science, maths, and history
     he knew;
His style at cricket was simply stunning
At rugger, soccer, hockey, running
     and swimming too.

The days went by, he grew mature;
He was a looker you may be sure,
     so straight
Old couples cried "God bless my soul
I thought that man was a telegraph pole"
     when he passed their gate.

His eyes were blue as a mountain lake,
He made the hearts of the girls to ache;
     he was strong;
He was gay, he was witty, his speaking voice
Sounded as if a large Rolls-Royce
     had passed along.

He kissed his dear old mater one day,
He said to her "I'm going away,
              good-bye".
No sword nor terrier by his side
He set off through the world so wide
              under the sky.

Where did he travel? Where didn't he travel?
Over the ice and over the gravel
              and the sea;
Up the fevered jungle river,
Through haunted forests without a shiver
              he wandered free.

What did he do? What didn't he do,
He rescued maidens, overthrew
              ten giants
Like factory chimneys, slaughtered dragons,
Though their heads were larger than railway waggons
              tamed their defiance.

What happened, what happened? I'm coming to that;
He came to a desert and down he sat
              and cried,
Above the blue sky arching wide
Two tall rocks as black as pride
              on either side.

There on a stone he sat him down,
Around the desert stretching brown
              like the tide,
Above the blue sky arching wide
Two black rocks on either side
              and, O how he cried.

"I thought my strength could know no stemming
  But I was foolish as a lemming;
          for what
  Was I born, was it only to see
  I'm as tired of life as life of me?
          let me be forgot.

"Children have heard of my every action
  It gives me no sort of satisfaction
          and why?
  Let me get this as clear as I possibly can
  No, I am not the truly strong man,
          O let me die."

There in the desert all alone
He sat for hours on a long flat stone
          and sighed;
Above the blue sky arching wide
Two black rocks on either side,
          and then he died.

Now ladies and gentlemen, big and small,
This story of course has a morale;
          again
Unless like him you wish to die
Listen, while my friend and I
          proceed to explain.

III

What had he done to be treated thus?
If you want to know, he'd offended us:
          for yes,
We guard the wells, we're handy with a gun,
We've a very special sense of fun,
          we curse and bless.

You are the town, and we are the clock,
We are the guardians of the gate in the rock,
      the Two;
On your left, and on your right
In the day, and in the night
      we are watching you.

Wiser not to ask just what has occurred
To them that disobeyed our word;
      to those
We were the whirlpool, we were the reef,
We were the formal nightmare, grief,
      and the unlucky rose.

Climb up the cranes, learn the sailors' words
When the ships from the islands, laden with birds
      come in;
Tell your stories of fishing and other men's wives,
The expansive moments of constricted lives,
      in the lighted inn.

By all means say of the peasant youth
"That person there is in the truth"
      we're kind,
Tire of your little rut and look it,
You have to obey but you don't have to like it,
      we do not mind:

But do not imagine we do not know
Or that what you hide with care won't show
      at a glance;
Nothing is done, nothing is said
But don't make the mistake of thinking us dead;
      I shouldn't dance

For I'm afraid in that case you'll have a fall;
We've been watching you over the garden wall
       for hours,
The sky is darkening like a stain,
Something is going to fall like rain
       and it won't be flowers.

When the green field comes off like a lid
Revealing what were much better hid,
       unpleasant;
And look! behind you without a sound
The woods have come up and are standing round
       in deadly crescent.

The bolt is sliding in its groove,
Outside the window is the black remov-
       ers' van,
And now with sudden swift emergence
Come the women in dark glasses, the hump-backed surgeons
       and the scissor-man.

This might happen any day
So be careful what you say
       or do
Be clean, be tidy, oil the lock,
Trim the garden, wind the clock:
       Remember the Two.

Song

Seen when night was silent,
The bean-shaped island

And our ugly comic servant
Who is observant

O the verandah and the fruit
   The tiny steamer in the bay
Startling summer with its hoot.
   You have gone away.

Who's Who

A shilling life will give you all the facts:
How Father beat him, how he ran away,
What were the struggles of his youth, what acts
Made him the greatest figure of his day:
Of how he fought, fished, hunted, worked all night,
Though giddy, climbed new mountains; named a sea:
Some of the last researchers even write
Love made him weep his pints like you and me.

With all his honours on, he sighed for one
Who, say astonished critics, lived at home;
Did little jobs about the house with skill
And nothing else; could whistle; would sit still
Or potter round the garden; answered some
Of his long marvellous letters but kept none.

Now Through Night's Caressing Grip

Now through night's caressing grip
Earth and all her oceans slip,
Capes of China slide away
From her fingers into day
And the Americas incline
Coasts towards her shadow line.
Now the ragged vagrants creep
Into crooked holes to sleep:
Just and unjust, worst and best,
Change their places as they rest:
Awkward lovers lie in fields
Where disdainful beauty yields:
While the splendid and the proud
Naked stand before the crowd
And the losing gambler gains
And the beggar entertains:
May sleep's healing power extend
Through these hours to our friend.
Unpursued by hostile force,
Traction engine, bull or horse
Or revolting succubus;
Calmly till the morning break
Let him lie, then gently wake.

In the Square

O for doors to be open and an invite with gilded edges
To dine with Lord Lobcock and Count Asthma on the
                                        platinum benches,
With the somersaults and fireworks, the roast and the
                                        smacking kisses—
        Cried the six cripples to the silent statue,
        The six beggared cripples.

And Garbo's and Cleopatra's wits to go astraying,
In a feather ocean with me to go fishing and playing
Still jolly when the cock has burst himself with crowing—
        Cried the six cripples to the silent statue,
        The six beggared cripples.

And to stand on green turf among the craning yellow faces,
Dependent on the chestnut, the sable, and Arabian horses,
And me with a magic crystal to foresee their places—
        Cried the six cripples to the silent statue,
        The six beggared cripples.

And this square to be a deck, and these pigeons sails to rig
And to follow the delicious breeze like a tantony pig
To the shaded feverless islands where the melons are big—
        Cried the six cripples to the silent statue,
        The six beggared cripples.

And these shops to be turned to tulips in a garden bed,
And me with my stick to thrash each merchant dead
As he pokes from a flower his bald and wicked head—
        Cried the six cripples to the silent statue,
        The six beggared cripples.

And a hole in the bottom of heaven, and Peter and Paul
And each smug surprised saint like parachutes to fall,
And every one-legged beggar to have no legs at all—
      Cried the six cripples to the silent statue,
      The six beggared cripples.

Madrigal

O lurcher-loving collier, black as night,
Follow your love across the smokeless hill;
Your lamp is out and all the cages still;
Course for her heart and do not miss,
For Sunday soon is past and, Kate, fly not so fast,
For Monday comes when none may kiss:
Be marble to his soot, and to his black be white.

Night Mail

(Commentary for a G.P.O. Film)

I

This is the Night Mail crossing the Border,
Bringing the cheque and the postal order,

Letters for the rich, letters for the poor,
The shop at the corner, the girl next door.

Pulling up Beattock, a steady climb:
The gradient's against her, but she's on time.

Past cotton-grass and moorland boulder,
Shovelling white steam over her shoulder,

Snorting noisily, she passes
Silent miles of wind-bent grasses.

Birds turn their heads as she approaches,
Stare from bushes at her blank-faced coaches.

Sheep-dogs cannot turn her course;
They slumber on with paws across.

In the farm she passes no one wakes,
But a jug in a bedroom gently shakes.

II

Dawn freshens. Her climb is done.
Down towards Glasgow she descends,
Towards the steam tugs yelping down a glade of cranes,
Towards the fields of apparatus, the furnaces
Set on the dark plain like gigantic chessmen.
All Scotland waits for her:
In dark glens, beside pale-green lochs,
Men long for news.

III

Letters of thanks, letters from banks,
Letters of joy from girl and boy,
Receipted bills and invitations
To inspect new stock or to visit relations,
And applications for situations,
And timid lovers' declarations,
And gossip, gossip from all the nations,
News circumstantial, news financial,
Letters with holiday snaps to enlarge in,
Letters with faces scrawled on the margin,
Letters from uncles, cousins and aunts,
Letters to Scotland from the South of France,
Letters of condolence to Highlands and Lowlands,
Written on paper of every hue,
The pink, the violet, the white and the blue,
The chatty, the catty, the boring, the adoring,
The cold and official and the heart's outpouring,
Clever, stupid, short and long,
The typed and the printed and the spelt all wrong.

IV

Thousands are still asleep,
Dreaming of terrifying monsters
Or a friendly tea beside the band in Cranston's or Crawford's:
Asleep in working Glasgow, asleep in well-set Edinburgh,
Asleep in granite Aberdeen,
They continue their dreams,
But shall wake soon and hope for letters,
And none will hear the postman's knock
Without a quickening of the heart.
For who can bear to feel himself forgotten?

Song

Let the florid music praise,
    The flute and the trumpet,
Beauty's conquest of your face:
In that land of flesh and bone,
Where from citadels on high
Her imperial standards fly,
    Let the hot sun
    Shine on, shine on.

O but the unloved have had power,
    The weeping and striking,
Always; time will bring their hour:
Their secretive children walk
Through your vigilance of breath
To unpardonable death,
    And my vows break
    Before his look.

Foxtrot from a Play

The soldier loves his rifle,
    The scholar loves his books,
The farmer loves his horses,
    The film star loves her looks.
There's love the whole world over
    Wherever you may be;
Some lose their rest for gay Mae West,
    But you're my cup of tea.

Some talk of Alexander
    And some of Fred Astaire,
Some like their heroes hairy
    Some like them debonair,
Some prefer a curate
    And some an A.D.C.,
Some like a tough to treat 'em rough,
    But you're my cup of tea.

Some are mad on Airedales
    And some on Pekinese,
On tabby cats or parrots
    Or guinea pigs or geese.
There are patients in asylums
    Who think that they're a tree;
I had an aunt who loved a plant,
    But you're my cup of tea.

Some have sagging waistlines
    And some a bulbous nose
And some a floating kidney
    And some have hammer toes,
Some have tennis elbow
    And some have housemaid's knee,
And some I know have got B.O.,
    But you're my cup of tea.

The blackbird loves the earthworm,
    The adder loves the sun,
The polar bear an iceberg,
    The elephant a bun,
The trout enjoys the river,
    The whale enjoys the sea,
And dogs love most an old lamp-post,
    But you're my cup of tea.

Underneath the Abject Willow

(For Benjamin Britten)

Underneath the abject willow,
    Lover, sulk no more;
Act from thought should quickly follow:
    What is thinking for?
Your unique and moping station
    Proves you cold;
    Stand up and fold
Your map of desolation.

Bells that toll across the meadows
    From the sombre spire,
Toll for those unloving shadows
    Love does not require.
All that lives may love; why longer
    Bow to loss
    With arms across?
Strike and you shall conquer.

Geese in flocks above you flying
    Their direction know;
Brooks beneath the thin ice flowing
    To their oceans go;
Coldest love will warm to action,
    Walk then, come,
    No longer numb,
Into your satisfaction.

Fish in the Unruffled Lakes

Fish in the unruffled lakes
The swarming colours wear,
Swans in the winter air
A white perfection have,
And the great lion walks
Through his innocent grove;
Lion, fish, and swan
Act, and are gone
Upon Time's toppling wave.

We till shadowed days are done,
We must weep and sing
Duty's conscious wrong,
The devil in the clock,
The Goodness carefully worn
For atonement or for luck;
We must lose our loves,
On each beast and bird that moves
Turn an envious look.

Sighs for folly said and done
Twist our narrow days;
But I must bless, I must praise
That you, my swan, who have
All gifts that to the swan
Impulsive Nature gave,
The majesty and pride,
Last night should add
Your voluntary love.

Song

      The chimney sweepers
Wash their faces and forget to wash the neck;
      The lighthouse keepers
Let the lamps go out and leave the ships to wreck;
      The prosperous baker
Leaves the rolls in hundreds in the oven to burn;
      The undertaker
Pins a small note on the coffin saying "Wait till I return,
      I've got a date with Love."

      And deep-sea divers
Cut their boots off and come bubbling to the top,
      And engine-drivers
Bring expresses in the tunnel to a stop;
      The village rector
Dashes down the side-aisle half-way through a psalm;
      The sanitary inspector
Runs off with the cover of the cesspool on his arm—
      To keep his date with Love.

At Last the Secret Is Out

At last the secret is out, as it always must come in the end,
The delicious story is ripe to tell to the intimate friend;
Over the tea-cups and in the square the tongue has its desire;
Still waters run deep, my dear, there's never smoke without fire.

Behind the corpse in the reservoir, behind the ghost on the links,
Behind the lady who dances and the man who madly drinks,
Under the look of fatigue, the attack of migraine and the sigh
There is always another story, there is more than meets the eye.

For the clear voice suddenly singing, high up in the convent wall,
The scent of the elder bushes, the sporting prints in the hall,
The croquet matches in summer, the handshake, the cough, the kiss,
There is always a wicked secret, a private reason for this.

Funeral Blues

Stop all the clocks, cut off the telephone,
Prevent the dog from barking with a juicy bone,
Silence the pianos and with muffled drum
Bring out the coffin, let the mourners come.

Let aeroplanes circle moaning overhead
Scribbling on the sky the message He Is Dead,
Put crêpe bows round the white necks of the public doves,
Let the traffic policemen wear black cotton gloves.

He was my North, my South, my East and West,
My working week and my Sunday rest,
My noon, my midnight, my talk, my song;
I thought that love would last for ever: I was wrong.

The stars are not wanted now; put out every one,
Pack up the moon and dismantle the sun,
Pour away the ocean and sweep up the wood;
For nothing now can ever come to any good.

Jam Tart

I'm a jam tart, I'm a bargain basement,
I'm a work of art, I'm a magic casement,
A coal cellar, an umbrella, a sewing machine,
A radio, a hymn book, an old french bean,
The Royal Scot, a fairy grot, a storm at sea, a tram—
　　　I don't know what I am,
　　　　You've cast a spell on me.

I'm a dog's nose, I'm Sir Humphry Davy,
I'm a Christmas rose, I'm the British Navy,
A motor, a bloater, a charcoal grill,
An octopus, a towpath, Hindenburg's will,
A village fair, a maiden's prayer, the B.B.C., a pram—
　　　I don't know what I am,
　　　　You've cast a spell on me.

I'm a salmon, I'm a starting pistol,
I'm backgammon, I'm the Port of Bristol.
A Times leader, a child's feeder, an aspirin,
The Ritz Hotel, a boy scout, the wages of sin,
A shaving brush, a schoolgirl's crush, the letter B, a ham—
　　　I don't know what I am,
　　　　You've cast a spell on me.

I'm an off-break, I'm a clump of beeches,
I'm a tummy ache, I'm Mussolini's speeches,
I'm Balmoral, I'm a sorrel mare, I'm a tug
A cigarette, an organ, a big bed-bug
A traffic sign, a rubber mine, a coffee tree, O damn—
　　　I don't know what I am,
　　　　You've cast a spell on me.

Death's Echo

"O who can ever gaze his fill,"
    Farmer and fisherman say,
"On native shore and local hill,
  Grudge aching limb or callus on the hand?
  Fathers, grandfathers stood upon this land,
  And here the pilgrims from our loins shall stand."
    So farmer and fisherman say
    In their fortunate heyday:
    But Death's soft answer drifts across
    Empty catch or harvest loss
      Or an unlucky May.

  The earth is an oyster with nothing inside it
    Not to be born is the best for man
  The end of toil is a bailiff's order
    Throw down the mattock and dance while you can.

"O life's too short for friends who share,"
    Travellers think in their hearts,
"The city's common bed, the air,
  The mountain bivouac and the bathing beach,
  Where incidents draw every day from each
  Memorable gesture and witty speech."
    So travellers think in their hearts,
    Till malice or circumstance parts
    Them from their constant humour:
    And shyly Death's coercive rumour
      In the silence starts.

  A friend is the old old tale of Narcissus
    Not to be born is the best for man
  An active partner in something disgraceful
    Change your partner, dance while you can.

"O stretch your hands across the sea,"
    The impassioned lover cries,
"Stretch them towards your harm and me.
  Our grass is green, and sensual our brief bed,
  The stream sings at its foot, and at its head
  The mild and vegetarian beasts are fed."
    So the impassioned lover cries
    Till his storm of pleasure dies:
    From the bedpost and the rocks
    Death's enticing echo mocks,
      And his voice replies.

The greater the love, the more false to its object
    Not to be born is the best for man
After the kiss comes the impulse to throttle
    Break the embraces, dance while you can.

"I see the guilty world forgiven,"
    Dreamer and drunkard sing,
"The ladders let down out of heaven;
  The laurel springing from the martyrs' blood;
  The children skipping where the weepers stood;
  The lovers natural, and the beasts all good."
    So dreamer and drunkard sing
    Till day their sobriety bring:
    Parrotwise with death's reply
    From whelping fear and nesting lie,
      Woods and their echoes ring.

The desires of the heart are as crooked as corkscrews
    Not to be born is the best for man
The second best is a formal order
    The dance's pattern, dance while you can.
Dance, dance, for the figure is easy
    The tune is catching and will not stop
Dance till the stars come down with the rafters
    Dance, dance, dance till you drop.

Letter to Lord Byron

PART I

Excuse, my lord, the liberty I take
    In thus addressing you. I know that you
Will pay the price of authorship and make
    The allowances an author has to do.
    A poet's fan-mail will be nothing new.
And then a lord—Good Lord, you must be peppered,
Like Gary Cooper, Coughlin, or Dick Sheppard,

With notes from perfect strangers starting, "Sir,
    I liked your lyrics, but *Childe Harold's* trash",
"My daughter writes, should I encourage her?"
    Sometimes containing frank demands for cash,
    Sometimes sly hints at a platonic pash,
And sometimes, though I think this rather crude,
The correspondent's photo in the rude.

And as for manuscripts—by every post . . .
    I can't improve on Pope's shrill indignation,
But hope that it will please his spiteful ghost
    To learn the use in culture's propagation
    Of modern methods of communication;
New roads, new rails, new contacts, as we know
From documentaries by the G.P.O.

For since the British Isles went Protestant
    A church confession is too high for most.
But still confession is a human want,
    So Englishmen must make theirs now by post
    And authors hear them over breakfast toast.
For, failing them, there's nothing but the wall
Of public lavatories on which to scrawl.

So if ostensibly I write to you
    To chat about your poetry or mine,
There're many other reasons; though it's true
    That I have, at the age of twenty-nine
    Just read *Don Juan* and I found it fine.
I read it on the boat to Reykjavik
Except when eating or asleep or sick.

The fact is, I'm in Iceland all alone
    —MacKenzie's prints are not unlike the scene—
Ich hab' zu Haus, ein Gra, ein Gramophone.
    Les gosses anglais aiment beaucoup les machines.
    Το καλον. glubit. che . . . what this may mean
I do not know, but rather like the sound
Of foreign languages like Ezra Pound.

And home is miles away, and miles away
    No matter who, and I am quite alone
And cannot understand what people say,
    But like a dog must guess it by the tone;
    At any language other than my own
I'm no great shakes, and here I've found no tutor
Nor sleeping lexicon to make me cuter.

The thought of writing came to me to-day
    (I like to give these facts of time and space);
The bus was in the desert on its way
    From Mothrudalur to some other place:
    The tears were streaming down my burning face;
I'd caught a heavy cold in Akureyri,
And lunch was late and life looked very dreary.

Professor Housman was I think the first
    To say in print how very stimulating
The little ills by which mankind is cursed,
    The colds, the aches, the pains are to creating;
    Indeed one hardly goes too far in stating
That many a flawless lyric may be due
Not to a lover's broken heart, but 'flu.

But still a proper explanation's lacking;
  Why write to you? I see I must begin
Right at the start when I was at my packing.
   The extra pair of socks, the airtight tin
   Of China tea, the anti-fly were in;
I asked myself what sort of books I'd read
In Iceland, if I ever felt the need.

I can't read Jefferies on the Wiltshire Downs,
  Nor browse on limericks in a smoking-room;
Who would try Trollope in cathedral towns,
  Or Marie Stopes inside his mother's womb?
  Perhaps you feel the same beyond the tomb.
Do the celestial highbrows only care
For works on Clydeside, Fascists, or Mayfair?

In certain quarters I had heard a rumour
  (For all I know the rumour's only silly)
That Icelanders have little sense of humour.
  I knew the country was extremely hilly,
  The climate unreliable and chilly;
So looking round for something light and easy
I pounced on you as warm and civilisé.

There is one other author in my pack:
  For some time I debated which to write to.
Which would least likely send my letter back?
  But I decided that I'd give a fright to
  Jane Austen if I wrote when I'd no right to,
And share in her contempt the dreadful fates
Of Crawford, Musgrove, and of Mr Yates.

Then she's a novelist. I don't know whether
  You will agree, but novel writing is
A higher art than poetry altogether
  In my opinion, and success implies
  Both finer character and faculties
Perhaps that's why real novels are as rare
As winter thunder or a polar bear.

The average poet by comparison
   Is unobservant, immature, and lazy.
You must admit, when all is said and done,
   His sense of other people's very hazy,
   His moral judgements are too often crazy,
A slick and easy generalisation
Appeals too well to his imagination.

I must remember, though, that you were dead
   Before the four great Russians lived, who brought
The art of novel writing to a head;
   The help of Boots had not been sought.
   But now the art for which Jane Austen fought,
Under the right persuasion bravely warms
And is the most prodigious of the forms.

She was not an unshockable blue-stocking;
   If shades remain the characters they were,
No doubt she still considers you as shocking.
   But tell Jane Austen, that is, if you dare,
   How much her novels are beloved down here.
She wrote them for posterity, she said;
'Twas rash, but by posterity she's read.

You could not shock her more than she shocks me;
   Beside her Joyce seems innocent as grass.
It makes me most uncomfortable to see
   An English spinster of the middle-class
   Describe the amorous effects of "brass",
Reveal so frankly and with such sobriety
The economic basis of society.

So it is you who is to get this letter.
   The experiment may not be a success.
There're many others who could do it better,
   But I shall not enjoy myself the less.
   Shaw of the Air Force said that happiness
Comes in absorption: he was right, I know it;
Even in scribbling to a long-dead poet.

Every exciting letter has enclosures,
    And so shall this—a bunch of photographs,
Some out of focus, some with wrong exposures,
    Press cuttings, gossip, maps, statistics, graphs;
    I don't intend to do the thing by halves.
I'm going to be very up to date indeed.
It is a collage that you're going to read.

I want a form that's large enough to swim in,
    And talk on any subject that I choose,
From natural scenery to men and women,
    Myself, the arts, the European news:
    And since she's on a holiday, my Muse
Is out to please, find everything delightful
And only now and then be mildly spiteful.

Ottava Rima would, I know, be proper,
    The proper instrument on which to pay
My compliments, but I should come a cropper;
    Rhyme-royal's difficult enough to play.
    But if no classics as in Chaucer's day,
At least my modern pieces shall be cheery
Like English bishops on the Quantum Theory.

Light verse, poor girl, is under a sad weather;
    Except by Milne and persons of that kind
She's treated as démodé altogether.
    It's strange and very unjust to my mind
    Her brief appearances should be confined,
Apart from Belloc's *Cautionary Tales,*
To the more bourgeois periodicals.

"The fascination of what's difficult,"
    The wish to do what one's not done before,
Is, I hope, proper to Quicunque Vult,
    The proper card to show at Heaven's door.
    "Gerettet" not "Gerichtet" be the Law,
Et cetera, et cetera. O curse,
That is the flattest line in English verse.

Parnassus after all is not a mountain,
    Reserved for A.1. climbers such as you;
It's got a park, it's got a public fountain.
        The most I ask is leave to share a pew
        With Bradford or with Cottam, that will do:
To pasture my few silly sheep with Dyer
And picnic on the lower slopes with Prior.

A publisher's an author's greatest friend,
    A generous uncle, or he ought to be.
(I'm sure we hope it pays him in the end.)
        I love my publishers and they love me,
        At least they paid a very handsome fee
To send me here. I've never heard a grouse
Either from Russell Square or Random House.

But now I've got uncomfortable suspicions,
    I'm going to put their patience out of joint.
Though it's in keeping with the best traditions
        For Travel Books to wander from the point
        (There is no other rhyme except anoint),
They well may charge me with—I've no defences—
Obtaining money under false pretences.

I know I've not the least chance of survival
    Beside the major travellers of the day.
I am no Lawrence who, on his arrival,
        Sat down and typed out all he had to say;
        I am not even Ernest Hemingway.
I shall not run to a two-bob edition,
So just won't enter for the competition.

And even here the steps I flounder in
    Were worn by most distinguished boots of old.
Dasent and Morris and Lord Dufferin,
        Hooker and men of that heroic mould
        Welcome me icily into the fold;
I'm not like Peter Fleming an Etonian,
But, if I'm Judas, I'm an old Oxonian.

The Haig Thomases are at Myvatn now,
    At Hvitavatn and at Vatnajökull
Cambridge research goes on, I don't know how:
    The shades of Asquith and of Auden Skökull
    Turn in their coffins a three-quarter circle
To see their son, upon whose help they reckoned,
Being as frivolous as Charles the Second.

So this, my opening chapter, has to stop
    With humbly begging everybody's pardon.
From Faber first in case the book's a flop,
    Then from the critics lest they should be hard on
    The author when he leads them up the garden,
Last from the general public he must beg
Permission now and then to pull their leg.

PART II

I'm writing this in pencil on my knee,
    Using my other hand to stop me yawning,
Upon a primitive, unsheltered quay
    In the small hours of a Wednesday morning.
    I cannot add the summer day is dawning;
In Seythisfjördur every schoolboy knows
That daylight in the summer never goes.

To get to sleep in latitudes called upper
    Is difficult at first for Englishmen.
It's like being sent to bed before your supper
    For playing darts with father's fountain-pen,
    Or like returning after orgies, when
Your breath's like luggage and you realise
You've been more confidential than was wise.

I've done my duty, taken many notes
            Upon the almost total lack of greenery,
The roads, the illegitimates, the goats:
            To use a rhyme of yours, there's handsome scenery
            But little agricultural machinery;
And with the help of Sunlight Soap the Geysir
Affords to visitors le plus grand plaisir.

The North, though, never was your cup of tea;
            "Moral" you thought it so you kept away.
And what I'm sure you're wanting now from me
            Is news about the England of the day,
            What sort of things La Jeunesse do and say.
Is Brighton still as proud of her pavilion,
And is it safe for girls to travel pillion?

I'll clear my throat and take a Rover's breath
            And skip a century of hope and sin—
For far too much has happened since your death.
            Crying went out and the cold bath came in,
            With drains, bananas, bicycles, and tin,
And Europe saw from Ireland to Albania
The Gothic revival and the Railway Mania.

We're entering now the Eotechnic Phase
            Thanks to the Grid and all those new alloys;
That is, at least, what Lewis Mumford says.
            A world of Aertex underwear for boys,
            Huge plate-glass windows, walls absorbing noise,
Where the smoke nuisance is utterly abated
And all the furniture is chromium-plated.

Well, you might think so if you went to Surrey
            And stayed for week-ends with the well to do,
Your car too fast, too personal your worry
            To look too closely at the wheeling view.
            But in the north it simply isn't true.
To those who live in Warrington or Wigan,
It's not a white lie, it's a whacking big 'un.

There on the old historic battlefield,
   The cold ferocity of human wills,
The scars of struggle are as yet unhealed;
   Slattern the tenements on sombre hills,
   And gaunt in valleys the square-windowed mills
That, since the Georgian house, in my conjecture
Remain our finest native architecture.

On economic, health, or moral grounds
   It hasn't got the least excuse to show;
No more than chamber pots or otter hounds:
   But let me say before it has to go,
   It's the most lovely country that I know;
Clearer than Scafell Pike, my heart has stamped on
The view from Birmingham to Wolverhampton.

Long, long ago, when I was only four,
   Going towards my grandmother, the line
Passed through a coal-field. From the corridor
   I watched it pass with envy, thought "How fine!
   Oh how I wish that situation mine."
Tramlines and slagheaps, pieces of machinery,
That was, and still is, my ideal scenery.

Hail to the New World! Hail to those who'll love
   Its antiseptic objects, feel at home.
Lovers will gaze at an electric stove,
   Another poésie de départ come
   Centred round bus-stops or the aerodrome.
But give me still, to stir imagination
The chiaroscuro of the railway station.

Preserve me from the Shape of Things to Be;
   The high-grade posters at the public meeting,
The influence of Art on Industry,
   The cinemas with perfect taste in seating;
   Preserve me, above all, from central heating.
It may be D. H. Lawrence hocus-pocus,
But I prefer a room that's got a focus.

But you want facts, not sighs. I'll do my best
    To give a few; you can't expect them all.
To start with, on the whole we're better dressed;
    For chic the difference to-day is small
    Of barmaid from my lady at the Hall.
It's sad to spoil this democratic vision
With millions suffering from malnutrition.

Again, our age is highly educated;
    There is no lie our children cannot read,
And as MacDonald might so well have stated
    We're growing up and up and up indeed.
    Advertisements can teach us all we need;
And death is better, as the millions know,
Than dandruff, night-starvation, or B.O.

We've always had a penchant for field sports,
    But what do you think has grown up in our towns?
A passion for the open air and shorts;
    The sun is one of our emotive nouns.
    Go down by chara' to the Sussex Downs,
Watch the manœuvres of the week-end hikers
Massed on parade with Kodaks or with Leicas.

These movements signify our age-long rule
    Of insularity has lost its powers;
The cult of salads and the swimming pool
    Comes from a climate sunnier than ours,
    And lands which never heard of licensed hours.
The south of England before very long
Will look no different from the Continong.

You lived and moved among the best society
    And so could introduce your hero to it
Without the slightest tremor of anxiety;
    Because he was your hero and you knew it,
    He'd know instinctively what's done, and do it.
He'd find our day more difficult than yours
For Industry has mixed the social drawers.

We've grown, you see, a lot more democratic,
　　And Fortune's ladder is for all to climb;
Carnegie on this point was most emphatic.
　　A humble grandfather is not a crime,
　　At least, if father made enough in time!
To-day, thank God, we've got no snobbish feeling
Against the more efficient modes of stealing.

The porter at the Carlton is my brother,
　　He'll wish me a good evening if I pay,
For tips and men are equal to each other.
　　I'm sure that *Vogue* would be the first to say
　　Que le Beau Monde is socialist to-day;
And many a bandit, not so gently born
Kills vermin every winter with the Quorn.

Adventurers, though, must take things as they find them
　　And look for pickings where the pickings are.
The drives of love and hunger are behind them,
　　They can't afford to be particular:
　　And those who like good cooking and a car,
A certain kind of costume or of face,
Must seek them in a certain kind of place.

Don Juan was a mixer and no doubt
　　Would find this century as good as any
For getting hostesses to ask him out,
　　And mistresses that need not cost a penny.
　　Indeed our ways to waste time are so many,
Thanks to technology, a list of these
Would make a longer book than *Ulysses*.

Yes, in the smart set he would know his way
　　By second nature with no tips from me.
Tennis and Golf have come in since your day;
　　But those who are as good at games as he
　　Acquire the back-hand quite instinctively,
Take to the steel-shaft and hole out in one,
Master the books of Ely Culbertson.

I see his face in every magazine.
      "Don Juan at lunch with one of Cochran's ladies."
"Don Juan with his red setter May MacQueen."
      "Don Juan, who's just been wintering in Cadiz,
      Caught at the wheel of his maroon Mercedes."
"Don Juan at Croydon Aerodrome." "Don Juan
Snapped in the paddock with the Agha Khan."

But if in highbrow circles he would sally
      It's just as well to warn him there's no stain on
Picasso, all-in-wrestling, or the Ballet.
      Sibelius is the man. To get a pain on
      Listening to Elgar is a sine qua non.
A second-hand acquaintance of Pareto's
Ranks higher than an intimate of Plato's.

The vogue for Black Mass and the cult of devils
      Has sunk. The Good, the Beautiful, the True
Still fluctuate about the lower levels.
      Joyces are firm and there there's nothing new.
      Eliots have hardened just a point or two.
Hopkins are brisk, thanks to some recent boosts.
There's been some further weakening in Prousts.

I'm saying this to tell you who's the rage,
      And not to loose a sneer from my interior.
Because there's snobbery in every age,
      Because some names are loved by the superior,
      It does not follow they're the least inferior:
For all I know the Beatific Vision's
On view at all Surrealist Exhibitions.

Now for the spirit of the people. Here
      I know I'm treading on more dangerous ground:
I know they're many changes in the air,
      But know my data too slight to be sound.
      I know, too, I'm inviting the renowned
Retort of all who love the Status Quo:
"You can't change human nature, don't you know!"

We've still, it's true, the same shape and appearance,
        We haven't changed the way that kissing's done;
The average man still hates all interference,
        Is just as proud still of his new-born son:
        Still, like a hen, he likes his private run,
Scratches for self-esteem, and slyly pecks
A good deal in the neighbourhood of sex.

But he's another man in many ways:
        Ask the cartoonist first, for he knows best.
Where is the John Bull of the good old days,
        The swaggering bully with the clumsy jest?
        His meaty neck has long been laid to rest,
His acres of self-confidence for sale;
He passed away at Ypres and Passchendaele.

Turn to the work of Disney or of Strube;
        There stands our hero in his threadbare seams;
The bowler hat who straphangs in the tube,
        And kicks the tyrant only in his dreams,
        Trading on pathos, dreading all extremes;
The little Mickey with the hidden grudge;
Which is the better, I leave you to judge.

Begot on Hire-Purchase by Insurance,
        Forms at his christening worshipped and adored;
A season ticket schooled him in endurance,
        A tax collector and a waterboard
        Admonished him. In boyhood he was awed
By a matric, and complex apparatuses
Keep his heart conscious of Divine Afflatuses.

"I am like you", he says, "and you, and you,
        I love my life, I love the home-fires, have
To keep them burning. Heroes never do.
        Heroes are sent by ogres to the grave.
        I may not be courageous, but I save.
I am the one who somehow turns the corner,
I may perhaps be fortunate Jack Horner.

"I am the ogre's private secretary;
     I've felt his stature and his powers, learned
To give his ogreship the raspberry
       Only when his gigantic back is turned.
       One day, who knows, I'll do as I have yearned.
The short man, all his fingers on the door,
With repartee shall send him to the floor."

One day, which day? O any other day,
     But not to-day. The ogre knows his man.
To kill the ogre—that would take away
       The fear in which his happy dreams began,
       And with his life he'll guard dreams while he can.
Those who would really kill his dream's contentment
He hates with real implacable resentment.

He dreads the ogre, but he dreads yet more
     Those who conceivably might set him free,
Those the cartoonist has no time to draw.
       Without his bondage he'd be all at sea;
       The ogre need but shout "Security",
To make this man, so loveable, so mild,
As madly cruel as a frightened child.

Byron, thou should'st be living at this hour!
     What would you do, I wonder, if you were?
Britannia's lost prestige and cash and power,
       Her middle classes show some wear and tear,
       We've learned to bomb each other from the air;
I can't imagine what the Duke of Wellington
Would say about the music of Duke Ellington.

Suggestions have been made that the Teutonic
     Führer-Prinzip would have appealed to you
As being the true heir to the Byronic—
       In keeping with your social status too
       (It has its English converts, fit and few),
That you would, hearing honest Oswald's call,
Be gleichgeschaltet in the Albert Hall.

"Lord Byron at the head of his storm-troopers!"
      Nothing, says science, is impossible:
The Pope may quit to join the Oxford Groupers,
      Nuffield may leave one farthing in his Will,
      There may be someone who trusts Baldwin still,
Someone may think that Empire wines are nice,
There may be people who hear Tauber twice.

You liked to be the centre of attention,
      The gay Prince Charming of the fairy story,
Who tamed the Dragon by his intervention.
      In modern warfare though it's just as gory,
      There isn't any individual glory;
The Prince must be anonymous, observant,
A kind of lab-boy, or a civil servant.

You never were an Isolationist;
      Injustice you had always hatred for,
And we can hardly blame you, if you missed
      Injustice just outside your lordship's door:
      Nearer than Greece were cotton and the poor.
To-day you might have seen them, might indeed
Have walked in the United Front with Gide,

Against the ogre, dragon, what you will;
      His many shapes and names all turn us pale,
For he's immortal, and to-day he still
      Swinges the horror of his scaly tail.
      Sometimes he seems to sleep, but will not fail
In every age to rear up to defend
Each dying force of history to the end.

Milton beheld him on the English throne,
      And Bunyan sitting in the Papal chair;
The hermits fought him in their caves alone,
      At the first Empire he was also there,
      Dangling his Pax Romana in the air:
He comes in dreams at puberty to man,
To scare him back to childhood if he can.

Banker or landlord, booking-clerk or Pope,
        Whenever he's lost faith in choice and thought,
When a man sees the future without hope,
        Whenever he endorses Hobbes' report
        "The life of man is nasty, brutish, short",
The dragon rises from his garden border
And promises to set up law and order.

He that in Athens murdered Socrates,
        And Plato then seduced, prepares to make
A desolation and to call it peace
        To-day for dying magnates, for the sake
        Of generals who can scarcely keep awake,
And for that doughy mass in great and small
That doesn't want to stir itself at all.

Forgive me for inflicting all this on you,
        For asking you to hold the baby for us;
It's easy to forget that where you've gone, you
        May only want to chat with Set and Horus,
        Bored to extinction with our earthly chorus:
Perhaps it sounds to you like a trunk-call,
Urgent, it seems, but quite inaudible.

Yet though the choice of what is to be done
        Remains with the alive, the rigid nation
Is supple still within the breathing one;
        Its sentinels yet keep their sleepless station,
        And every man in every generation,
Tossing in his dilemma on his bed,
Cries to the shadows of the noble dead.

We're out at sea now, and I wish we weren't;
        The sea is rough, I don't care if it's blue;
I'd like to have a quick one, but I daren't.
        And I must interrupt this screed to you,
        For I've some other little jobs to do;
I must write home or mother will be vexed,
So this must be continued in our next.

PART III

My last remarks were sent you from a boat.
    I'm back on shore now in a warm bed-sitter,
And several friends have joined me since I wrote;
    So though the weather out of doors is bitter,
    I feel a great deal cheerier and fitter.
A party from a public school, a poet,
Have set a rapid pace, and make me go it.

We're starting soon on a big expedition
    Into the desert, which I'm sure is corking:
Many would like to be in my position.
    I only hope there won't be too much walking.
    Now let me see, where was I? We were talking
Of Social Questions when I had to stop;
I think it's time now for a little shop.

In setting up my brass-plate as a critic,
    I make no claim to certain diagnosis,
I'm more intuitive than analytic,
    I offer thought in homeopathic doses
    (But someone may get better in the process).
I don't pretend to reasoning like Pritchard's
Or the logomachy of I. A. Richards.

I like your muse because she's gay and witty,
    Because she's neither prostitute nor frump,
The daughter of a European city,
    And country houses long before the slump;
    I like her voice that does not make me jump:
And you I find sympatisch, a good townee,
Neither a preacher, ninny, bore, nor Brownie.

A poet, swimmer, peer, and man of action,
 —It beats Roy Campbell's record by a mile—
You offer every possible attraction.
        By looking into your poetic style,
        And love-life on the chance that both were vile,
Several have earned a decent livelihood,
Whose lives were uncreative but were good.

You've had your packet from the critics, though:
        They grant you warmth of heart, but at your head
Their moral and aesthetic brickbats throw.
        A "vulgar genius" so George Eliot said,
        Which doesn't matter as George Eliot's dead,
But T. S. Eliot, I am sad to find,
Damns you with: "an uninteresting mind".

A statement which I must say I'm ashamed at;
        A poet must be judged by his intention,
And serious thought you never said you aimed at.
        I think a serious critic ought to mention
        That one verse style was really your invention,
A style whose meaning does not need a spanner,
You are the master of the airy manner.

By all means let us touch our humble caps to
        La poésie pure, the epic narrative;
But comedy shall get its round of claps, too.
        According to his powers, each may give;
        Only on varied diet can we live.
The pious fable and the dirty story
Share in the total literary glory.

There's every mode of singing robe in stock,
        From Shakespeare's gorgeous fur coat, Spenser's muff,
Or Dryden's lounge suit to my cotton frock,
        And Wordsworth's Harris tweed with leathern cuff.
        Firbank, I think, wore just a just-enough;
I fancy Whitman in a reach-me-down,
But you, like Sherlock, in a dressing-gown.

I'm also glad to find I've your authority
      For finding Wordsworth a most bleak old bore,
Though I'm afraid we're in a sad minority
      For every year his followers get more,
      Their number must have doubled since the war.
They come in train-loads to the Lakes, and swarms
Of pupil-teachers study him in *Storm*'s.

"I hate a pupil-teacher" Milton said,
      Who also hated bureaucratic fools;
Milton may thank his stars that he is dead,
      Although he's learnt by heart in public schools,
      Along with Wordsworth and the list of rules;
For many a don while looking down his nose
Calls Pope and Dryden classics of our prose.

And new plants flower from that old potato.
      They thrive best in a poor industrial soil,
Are hardier crossed with Rousseaus or a Plato;
      Their cultivation is an easy toil.
      William, to change the metaphor, struck oil;
His well seems inexhaustible, a gusher
That saves old England from the fate of Russia.

The mountain-snob is a Wordsworthian fruit;
      He tears his clothes and doesn't shave his chin,
He wears a very pretty little boot,
      He chooses the least comfortable inn;
      A mountain railway is a deadly sin;
His strength, of course, is as the strength of ten men,
He calls all those who live in cities wen-men.

I'm not a spoil-sport, I would never wish
      To interfere with anybody's pleasures;
By all means climb, or hunt, or even fish,
      All human hearts have ugly little treasures;
      But think it time to take repressive measures
When someone says, adopting the "I know" line,
The Good Life is confined above the snow-line.

Besides, I'm very fond of mountains, too;
    I like to travel through them in a car;
I like a house that's got a sweeping view;
    I like to walk, but not to walk too far.
    I also like green plains where cattle are,
And trees and rivers, and shall always quarrel
With those who think that rivers are immoral.

Not that my private quarrel gives quietus to
    The interesting question that it raises;
Impartial thought will give a proper status to
    This interest in waterfalls and daisies,
    Excessive love for the non-human faces,
That lives in hearts from Golders Green to Teddington;
It's all bound up with Einstein, Jeans, and Eddington.

It is a commonplace that's hardly worth
    A poet's while to make profound or terse,
That now the sun does not go round the earth,
    That man's no centre of the universe;
    And working in an office makes it worse.
The humblest is acquiring with facility
A Universal-Complex sensibility.

For now we've learnt we mustn't be so bumptious
    We find the stars are one big family,
And send out invitations for a scrumptious
    Simple, old-fashioned, jolly romp with tea
    To any natural objects we can see.
We can't, of course, invite a Jew or Red
But birds and nebulae will do instead.

The Higher Mind's outgrowing the Barbarian,
    It's hardly thought hygienic now to kiss;
The world is surely turning vegetarian;
    And as it grows too sensitive for this.
    It won't be long before we find there is
A Society of Everybody's Aunts
For the Prevention of Cruelty to Plants.

I dread this like the dentist, rather more so:
     To me Art's subject is the human clay,
And landscape but a background to a torso;
     All Cézanne's apples I would give away
     For one small Goya or a Daumier.
I'll never grant a more than minor beauty
To pudge or pilewort, petty-chap or pooty.

Art, if it doesn't start there, at least ends,
     Whether aesthetics like the thought or not,
In an attempt to entertain our friends;
     And our first problem is to realise what
     Peculiar friends the modern artist's got;
It's possible a little dose of history
May help us in unravelling this mystery.

At the Beginning I shall *not* begin,
     Not with the scratches in the ancient caves;
Heard only knows the latest bulletin
     About the finds in the Egyptian graves;
     I'll skip the war-dance of the Indian braves;
Since, for the purposes I have in view,
The English eighteenth century will do.

We find two arts in the Augustan age:
     One quick and graceful, and by no means holy,
Relying on his lordship's patronage;
     The other pious, sober, moving slowly,
     Appealing mainly to the poor and lowly.
So Isaac Watts and Pope, each forced his entry
To lower middle class and landed gentry.

Two arts as different as Jews and Turks,
     Each serving aspects of the Reformation,
Luther's division into faith and works:
     The God of the unique imagination,
     A friend of those who have to know their station;
And the Great Architect, the Engineer
Who keeps the mighty in their higher sphere.

The important point to notice, though, is this:
  Each poet knew for whom he had to write,
Because their life was still the same as his.
    As long as art remains a parasite,
    On any class of persons it's alright;
The only thing it must be is attendant,
The only thing it mustn't, independent.

But artists, though, are human; and for man
  To be a scivvy is not nice at all:
So everyone will do the best he can
    To get a patch of ground which he can call
    His own. He doesn't really care how small,
So long as he can style himself the master:
Unluckily for art, it's a disaster.

To be a highbrow is the natural state:
  To have a special interest of one's own,
Rock gardens, marrows, pigeons, silver plate,
    Collecting butterflies or bits of stone;
    And then to have a circle where one's known
Of hobbyists and rivals to discuss
With expert knowledge what appeals to us.

But to the artist this is quite forbidden:
  On this point he must differ from the crowd,
And, like a secret agent, must keep hidden
    His passion for his shop. However proud,
    And rightly, of his trade, he's not allowed
To etch his face with his professional creases,
Or die from occupational diseases.

Until the great Industrial Revolution
  The artist had to earn his livelihood:
However much he hated the intrusion
    Of patron's taste or public's fickle mood,
    He had to please or go without his food;
He had to keep his technique to himself
Or find no joint upon his larder shelf.

But Savoury and Newcomen and Watt
    And all those names that I was told to get up
In history preparation and forgot,
    A new class of creative artist set up,
      On whom the pressure of demand was let up:
He sang and painted and drew dividends,
But lost responsibilities and friends.

Those most affected were the very best:
    Those with originality of vision,
Those whose technique was better than the rest,
    Jumped at the chance of a secure position
      With freedom from the bad old hack tradition,
Leave to be sole judges of the artist's brandy,
Be Shelley, or Childe Harold, or the Dandy.

So started what I'll call the Poet's Party:
    (Most of the guests were painters, never mind)—
The first few hours the atmosphere was hearty,
    With fireworks, fun, and games of every kind;
      All were enjoying it, no one was blind;
Brilliant the speeches improvised, the dances,
And brilliant, too, the technical advances.

How nice at first to watch the passers-by
    Out of the upper window, and to say
"How glad I am that though I have to die
    Like all those cattle, I'm less base than they!"
      How we all roared when Baudelaire went fey.
"See this cigar", he said, "it's Baudelaire's.
What happens to perception? Ah, who cares?"

To-day, alas, that happy crowded floor
    Looks very different: many are in tears:
Some have retired to bed and locked the door;
    And some swing madly from the chandeliers;
      Some have passed out entirely in the rears;
Some have been sick in corners; the sobering few
Are trying hard to think of something new.

I've made it seem the artist's silly fault,
    In which case why these sentimental sobs?
In fact, of course, the whole tureen was salt.
        The soup was full of little bits of snobs.
        The common clay and the uncommon nobs
Were far too busy making piles or starving
To look at pictures, poetry, or carving.

I've simplified the facts to be emphatic,
    Playing Macaulay's favourite little trick
Of lighting that's contrasted and dramatic;
        Because it's true Art feels a trifle sick,
        You mustn't think the old girl's lost her kick.
And those, besides, who feel most like a sewer
Belong to Painting not to Literature.

You know the terror that for poets lurks
    Beyond the ferry when to Minos brought.
Poets must utter their Collected Works,
        Including Juvenilia. So I thought
        That you might warn him. Yes, I think you ought,
In case, when my turn comes, he shall cry "Atta boys,
Off with his bags, he's crazy as a hatter, boys!"

The clock is striking and it's time for lunch;
    We start at four. The weather's none too bright.
Some of the party look as pleased as Punch.
        We shall be travelling, as they call it, light;
        We shall be sleeping in a tent to-night.
You know what Baden-Powell's taught us, don't you,
Ora pro nobis, please, this evening, won't you?

PART IV

A ship again; this time the *Dettifoss*.
　　Grierson can buy it; all the sea I mean,
All this Atlantic that we've now to cross
　　Heading for England's pleasant pastures green.
　　Pro tem I've done with the Icelandic scene;
I watch the hills receding in the distance,
I hear the thudding of an engine's pistons.

I hope I'm better, wiser for the trip:
　　I've had the benefit of northern breezes,
The open road and good companionship,
　　I've seen some very pretty little pieces;
　　And though the luck was almost all MacNeice's,
I've spent some jolly evenings playing rummy—
No one can talk at Bridge, unless it's Dummy.

I've learnt to ride, at least to ride a pony,
　　Taken a lot of healthy exercise,
On barren mountains and in valleys stony,
　　I've tasted a hot spring (a taste was wise),
　　And foods a man remembers till he dies.
All things considered, I consider Iceland,
Apart from Reykjavik, a very nice land.

The part can stand as symbol for the whole:
　　So ruminating in these last few weeks,
I see the map of all my youth unroll,
　　The mental mountains and the psychic creeks,
　　The towns of which the master never speaks,
The various parishes and what they voted for,
The colonies, their size, and what they're noted for.

A child may ask when our strange epoch passes,
　　During a history lesson, "Please, sir, what's
An intellectual of the middle classes?
　　Is he a maker of ceramic pots
　　Or does he choose his king by drawing lots?"
What follows now may set him on the rail,
A plain, perhaps a cautionary, tale.

My passport says I'm five feet and eleven,
　　With hazel eyes and fair (it's tow-like) hair,
That I was born in York in 1907,
　　With no distinctive markings anywhere.
　　Which isn't quite correct. Conspicuous there
On my right cheek appears a large brown mole,
I think I don't dislike it on the whole.

My name occurs in several of the sagas,
　　Is common over Iceland still. Down under
Where Das Volk order sausages and lagers
　　I ought to be the prize, the living wonder,
　　The really pure from any Rassenschander,
In fact I am the great big white barbarian,
The Nordic type, the too too truly Aryan.

In games which mark for beauty out of twenty,
　　I'm doing well if my friends give me eight
(When played historically you still score plenty);
　　My head looks like an egg upon a plate;
　　My nose is not too bad, but isn't straight;
I have no proper eyebrows, and my eyes
Are far too close together to look nice.

Beauty, we're told, is but a painted show,
　　But still the public really likes that best;
Beauty of soul should be enough, I know,
　　The golden ingot in the plain deal chest.
　　But mine's a rattle in a flannel vest;
I can't think what my It had on It's mind,
To give me flat feet and a big behind.

Apart from lyrics and poetic dramma,
　　Which Ervine seems more angered by than sad at,
While Sparrow fails to understand their grammar,
　　I have some harmless hobbies; I'm not bad at
　　Reading the slower movements, and may add that
Out of my hours of strumming most of them
Pass playing hymn tunes out of A. and M.

Read character from taste. Who seem to me
　　The great? I know that one as well as you.
"Why, Daunty, Gouty, Shopkeeper, the three
　　Supreme Old Masters." You must ask me who
　　Have written just as I'd have liked to do.
I stop to listen and the names I hear
Are those of Firbank, Potter, Carroll, Lear.

Then phantasies? My anima, poor thing,
　　Must take the dreams my Alter Ego sends her,
And he's a marvellous diver, not a king.
　　But when I'm sickening for influenza,
　　I play concertos with my own cadenza;
And as the fever rises find it properer
To sing the love duet from a grand opera.

My vices? I've no wish to go to prison.
　　I am no Grouper, I will never share
With any prig who thinks he'd like to listen.
　　At answering letters I am well aware
　　I'm very slack; I ought to take more care
Over my clothes; my promise always fails
To smoke much less, and not to bite my nails.

I hate pompositas and all authority;
　　Its air of injured rightness also sends
Me shuddering from the cultured smug minority.
　　"Perpetual revolution", left-wing friends
　　Tell me, "in counter-revolution ends.
Your fate will be to linger on outcast
A selfish pink old Liberal to the last."

"No, I am that I am, and those that level
     At my abuses reckon up their own.
I may be straight though they, themselves, are bevel."
          So Shakespeare said, but Shakespeare must have known.
          I daren't say that except when I'm alone,
Must hear in silence till I turn my toes up,
"It's such a pity Wystan never grows up."

So I sit down this fine September morning
     To tell my story. I've another reason.
I've lately had a confidential warning
          That Isherwood is publishing next season
          A book about us all. I call that treason.
I must be quick if I'm to get my oar in
Before his revelations bring the law in.

My father's forbears were all Midland yeomen
     Till royalties from coal mines did them good;
I think they must have been phlegmatic slowmen.
          My mother's ancestors had Norman blood,
          From Somerset I've always understood;
My grandfathers on either side agree
In being clergymen and C. of E.

Father and Mother each was one of seven,
     Though one died young and one was not all there;
Their fathers both went suddenly to Heaven
          While they were still quite small and left them here
          To work on earth with little cash to spare;
A nurse, a rising medico, at Bart's
Both felt the pangs of Cupid's naughty darts.

My home then was professional and "high".
     No gentler father ever lived, I'll lay
All Lombard Street against a shepherd's pie.
          We imitate our loves: well, neighbours say
          I grow more like my mother every day.
I don't like business men. I know a Prot
Will never really kneel, but only squat.

In pleasures of the mind they both delighted;
    The library in the study was enough
To make a better boy than me short-sighted;
        Our old cook Ada surely knew her stuff;
        My elder brothers did not treat me rough;
We lived at Solihull, a village then;
Those at the gasworks were my favourite men.

My earliest recollection to stay put
    Is of a white stone doorstep and a spot
Of pus where father lanced the terrier's foot;
        Next, stuffing shag into the coffee pot
        Which nearly killed my mother, but did not;
Both psycho–analyst and Christian minister,
Will think these incidents extremely sinister.

With northern myths my little brain was laden,
    With deeds of Thor and Loki and such scenes;
My favourite tale was Andersen's *Ice Maiden;*
        But better far than any kings or queens
        I liked to see and know about machines:
And from my sixth until my sixteenth year
I thought myself a mining engineer.

The mine I always pictured was for lead,
    Though copper mines might, faute de mieux, be sound.
To-day I like a weight upon my bed;
        I always travel by the Underground;
        For concentration I have always found
A small room best, the curtains drawn, the light on;
Then I can work from nine till tea-time, right on.

I must admit that I was most precocious
    (Precocious children rarely grow up good).
My aunts and uncles thought me quite atrocious
        For using words more adult than I should;
        My first remark at school did all it could
To shake a matron's monumental poise;
"I like to see the various types of boys."

The Great War had begun: but masters' scrutiny
       And fists of big boys were the war to us;
It was as harmless as the Indian Mutiny,
       A beating from the Head was dangerous.
       But once when half the form put down *Bellus.*
We were accused of that most deadly sin,
Wanting the Kaiser and the Huns to win.

The way in which we really were affected
       Was having such a varied lot to teach us.
The best were fighting, as the King expected,
       The remnant either elderly grey creatures,
       Or characters with most peculiar features.
Many were raggable, a few were waxy,
One had to leave abruptly in a taxi.

Surnames I must not write—O Reginald,
       You at least taught us that which fadeth not,
Our earliest visions of the great wide world;
       The beer and biscuits that your favourites got,
       Your tales revealing you a first-class shot,
Your riding breeks, your drama called *The Waves,*
A few of us will carry to our graves.

"Half a lunatic, half a knave". No doubt
       A holy terror to the staff at tea;
A good headmaster must have soon found out
       Your moral character was all at sea;
       I question if you'd got a pass degree:
But little children bless your kind that knocks
Away the edifying stumbling blocks.

How can I thank you? For it only shows
       (Let me ride just this once my hobby-horse),
There're things a good headmaster never knows.
       There must be sober schoolmasters, of course,
       But what a prep school really puts across
Is knowledge of the world we'll soon be lost in:
To-day it's more like Dickens than Jane Austen.

I hate the modern trick, to tell the truth,
        Of straightening out the kinks in the young mind,
Our passion for the tender plant of youth,
        Our hatred for all weeds of any kind.
        Slogans are bad: the best that I can find
Is this: "Let each child have that's in our care
As much neurosis as the child can bear."

In this respect, at least, my bad old Adam is
        Pigheadedly against the general trend;
And has no use for all these new academies
        Where readers of the better weeklies send
        The child they probably did not intend,
To paint a lampshade, marry, or keep pigeons,
Or make a study of the world religions.

Goddess of bossy underlings, Normality!
        What murders are committed in thy name!
Totalitarian is thy state Reality,
        Reeking of antiseptics and the shame
        Of faces that all look and feel the same.
Thy Muse is one unknown to classic histories,
The topping figure of the hockey mistress.

From thy dread Empire not a soul's exempted:
        More than the nursemaids pushing prams in parks,
By thee the intellectuals are tempted,
        O, to commit the treason of the clerks,
        Bewitched by thee to literary sharks.
But I must leave thee to thy office stool,
I must get on now to my public school.

Men had stopped throwing stones at one another,
        Butter and Father had come back again;
Gone were the holidays we spent with Mother
        In furnished rooms on mountain, moor, and fen;
        And gone those summer Sunday evenings, when
Along the seafronts fled a curious noise,
"Eternal Father", sung by three young boys.

Nation spoke Peace, or said she did, with nation;
     The sexes tried their best to look the same;
Morals lost value during the inflation,
     The great Victorians kindly took the blame;
     Visions of Dada to the Post-War came,
Sitting in cafés, nostrils stuffed with bread,
Above the recent and the straight-laced dead.

I've said my say on public schools elsewhere:
     Romantic friendship, prefects, bullying,
I shall not deal with, c'est une autre affaire.
     Those who expect them, will get no such thing,
     It is the strictly relevant I sing.
Why should they grumble? They've the Greek Anthology,
And all the spicier bits of Anthropology.

We all grow up the same way, more or less;
     Life is not known to give away her presents;
She only swops. The unself-consciousness
     That children share with animals and peasants
     Sinks in the *Sturm und Drang* of Adolescence.
Like other boys I lost my taste for sweets,
Discovered sunsets, passion, God, and Keats.

I shall recall a single incident
     No more. I spoke of mining engineering
As the career on which my mind was bent,
     But for some time my fancies had been veering;
     Mirages of the future kept appearing;
Crazes had come and gone in short, sharp gales,
For motor-bikes, photography, and whales.

But indecision broke off with a clean-cut end
     One afternoon in March at half-past three
When walking in a ploughed field with a friend;
     Kicking a little stone, he turned to me
     And said, "Tell me, do you write poetry?"
I never had, and said so, but I knew
That very moment what I wished to do.

Without a bridge passage this leads me straight
        Into the theme marked "Oxford" on my score
From pages twenty-five to twenty-eight.
        Aesthetic trills I'd never heard before
        Rose from the strings, shrill poses from the cor;
The woodwind chattered like a pre-war Russian,
"Art" boomed the brass, and "Life" thumped the percussion.

A raw provincial, my good taste was tardy,
        And Edward Thomas I as yet preferred;
I was still listening to Thomas Hardy
        Putting divinity about a bird;
        But Eliot spoke the still unspoken word;
For gasworks and dried tubers I forsook
The clock at Grantchester, the English rook.

All youth's intolerant certainty was mine as
        I faced life in a double-breasted suit;
I bought and praised but did not read Aquinas,
        At the *Criterion's* verdict I was mute,
        Though Arnold's I was ready to refute;
And through the quads dogmatic words rang clear,
"Good poetry is classic and austere."

So much for Art. Of course Life had its passions too;
        The student's flesh like his imagination
Makes facts fit theories and has fashions too.
        We were the tail, a sort of poor relation
        To that debauched, eccentric generation
That grew up with their fathers at the War,
And made new glosses on the noun Amor.

Three years passed quickly while the Isis went
        Down to the sea for better or for worse;
Then to Berlin, not Carthage, I was sent
        With money from my parents in my purse,
        And ceased to see the world in terms of verse.
I met a chap called Layard and he fed
New doctrines into my receptive head.

Part came from Lane, and part from D. H. Lawrence;
    Gide, though I didn't know it then, gave part.
They taught me to express my deep abhorrence
    If I caught anyone preferring Art
    To Life and Love and being Pure-in-Heart.
I lived with crooks but seldom was molested;
The Pure-in-Heart can never be arrested.

He's gay; no bludgeonings of chance can spoil it,
    The Pure-in-Heart loves all men on a par,
And has no trouble with his private toilet;
    The Pure-in-Heart is never ill; catarrh
    Would be the yellow streak, the brush of tar;
Determined to be loving and forgiving,
I came back home to try and earn my living.

The only thing you never turned your hand to
    Was teaching English in a boarding school.
To-day it's a profession that seems grand to
    Those whose alternative's an office stool;
    For budding authors it's become the rule.
To many an unknown genius postmen bring
Typed notices from Rabbitarse and String.

The Head's M.A., a bishop is a patron,
    The assistant staff is highly qualified;
Health is the care of an experienced matron,
    The arts are taught by ladies from outside;
    The food is wholesome and the grounds are wide;
The aim is training character and poise,
With special coaching for the backward boys.

I found the pay good and had time to spend it,
    Though others may not have the good luck I did:
For you I'd hesitate to recommend it;
    Several have told me that they can't abide it.
    Still, if one tends to get a bit one-sided,
It's pleasant as it's easy to secure
The hero worship of the immature.

More, it's a job, and jobs to-day are rare:
        All the ideals in the world won't feed us
Although they give our crimes a certain air.
        So barons of the press who know their readers
        Employ to write their more appalling leaders,
Instead of Satan's horned and hideous minions,
Clever young men of liberal opinions.

Which brings me up to nineteen-thirty-five;
        Six months of film work is another story
I can't tell now. But, here I am, alive
        Knowing the true source of that sense of glory
        That still surrounds the England of the Tory,
Come only to the rather tame conclusion
That no man by himself has life's solution.

I know—the fact is really not unnerving—
        That what is done is done, that no past dies,
That what we see depends on who's observing,
        And what we think on our activities.
        That envy warps the virgin as she dries
But "Post coitum, homo tristis" means
The lover must go carefully with the greens.

The boat has brought me to the landing-stage,
        Up the long estuary of mud and sedges;
The line I travel has the English gauge;
        The engine's shadow vaults the little hedges;
        And summer's done. I sign the usual pledges
To be a better poet, better man;
I'll really do it this time if I can.

I'm home again, and goodness knows to what,
        To read the papers and to earn my bread;
I'm home to Europe where I may be shot;
        "I'm home again", as William Morris said,
        "And nobody I really care for's dead."
I've got a round of visits now to pay,
So I must finish this another day.

PART V

Autumn is here. The beech leaves strew the lawn;
    The power stations take up heavier loads;
The massive lorries shake from dusk till dawn
    The houses on the residential roads;
    The shops are full of coming winter modes.
Dances have started at the Baths next door
Stray scraps of MS strew my bedroom floor.

I read that there's a boomlet on in Birmingham,
    But what I hear is not so reassuring;
Rumours of War, the B.B.C. confirming 'em,
    The prospects for the future aren't alluring;
    No one believes Prosperity enduring,
Not even Wykehamists, whose golden mean
Maintains the All Souls' Parish Magazine.

The crack between employees and employers
    Is obvious already as the nose on
John Gielgud's face; the keels of new destroyers
    Get laid down somehow though all credit's frozen;
    The Pope's turned protestant at last and chosen,
Thinking it safer in the temporal circs,
The Italian faith against the Russian works.

England, my England—you have been my tutrix—
    The Mater, on occasions, of the free,
Or, if you'd rather, Dura Virum Nutrix,
    Whatever happens I am born of Thee;
    And Englishmen, all foreigners agree,
Taking them by and large, and as a nation,
All suffer from an Oedipus fixation.

With all thy faults, of course we love thee still;
        We'd better for we have to live with you,
From Rhondda Valley or from Bredon Hill,
        From Rotherhithe, or Regent Street, or Kew
        We look you up and down and whistle "Phew!
Mother looks odd to-day dressed up in peers,
Slums, aspidistras, shooting-sticks, and queers."

Cheer up! There're several singing birds that sing.
        There's six feet six of Spender for a start;
Eliot has really stretched his eagle's wing,
        And Yeats has helped himself to Parnell's heart;
        This book has samples of MacNeice's art;
There's Wyndham Lewis fuming out of sight,
That lonely old volcano of the Right.

I'm marking time because I cannot guess
        The proper place to which to send this letter,
c/o Saint Peter or The Infernal Press?
        I'll try the Press. World-culture is its debtor;
        It has a list that Faber's couldn't better.
For Heaven gets all the lookers for her pains,
But Hell, I think, gets nearly all the brains.

The congregation up there in the former
        Are those whose early upbringing was right,
Who never suffered from a childish trauma;
        As babies they were Truby King's delight;
        They're happy, lovely, but not overbright.
For no one thinks unless a complex makes him,
Or till financial ruin overtakes him.

Complex or Poverty; in short The Trap.
        Some set to work to understand the spring;
Others sham dead, pretend to take a nap;
        "It is a motor-boat," the madmen sing;
        The artist's action is the queerest thing:
He seems to like it, couldn't do without it,
And only wants to tell us all about it.

While Rome is burning or he's out of sorts
        "Causons, causons, mon bon," he's apt to say,
"What does it matter while I have these thoughts?"
        Or so I've heard, but Freud's not quite O.K.
        No artist works a twenty-four hour day.
In bed, asleep or dead, it's hard to tell
The highbrow from l'homme moyen sensuel.

"Es neigen die Weisen zu Schönem sich."
        Your lordship's brow that never wore a hat
Should thank your lordship's foot that did the trick.
        Your mother in a temper cried, "Lame Brat!"
        Posterity should thank her much for that.
Had she been sweet she surely would have taken
Juan away and saved your moral bacon.

The match of Hell and Heaven was a nice
        Idea of Blake's, but won't take place, alas.
You can choose either, but you can't choose twice;
        You can't, at least in this world, change your class;
        Neither is alpha plus though both will pass:
And don't imagine you can write like Dante,
Dive like your nephew, crochet like your auntie.

The Great Utopia, free of all complexes,
        The Withered State is, at the moment, such
A dream as that of being both the sexes.
        I like Wolf's *Goethe-Lieder* very much,
        But doubt if *Ganymede*'s appeal will touch
—That marvellous cry with its ascending phrases—
Capitalism in its later phases.

Are Poets saved? Well, let's suppose they are,
        And take a peep. I don't see any books.
Shakespeare is lounging grandly at the bar,
        Milton is dozing, judging by his looks,
        Shelley is playing poker with two crooks,
Blake's adding pince-nez to an ad. for players,
Chaucer is buried in the latest Sayers.

Lord Alfred rags with Arthur on the floor,
      Housman, all scholarship forgot at last,
Sips up the stolen waters through a straw,
      Browning's complaining that Keats bowls too fast,
      And you have been composing as they passed
A clerihew on Wordsworth and his tie,
A rather dirty limerick on Pye.

I hope this reaches you in your abode,
      This letter that's already far too long,
Just like the Prelude or the Great North Road;
      But here I end my conversational song.
      I hope you don't think mail from strangers wrong.
As to its length, I tell myself you'll need it,
You've all eternity in which to read it.

Lullaby

Lay your sleeping head, my love,
Human on my faithless arm;
Time and fevers burn away
Individual beauty from
Thoughtful children, and the grave
Proves the child ephemeral:
But in my arms till break of day
Let the living creature lie,
Mortal, guilty, but to me
The entirely beautiful.

Soul and body have no bounds:
To lovers as they lie upon
Her tolerant enchanted slope
In their ordinary swoon,
Grave the vision Venus sends
Of supernatural sympathy,
Universal love and hope;
While an abstract insight wakes
Among the glaciers and the rocks
The hermit's sensual ecstasy.

Certainty, fidelity
On the stroke of midnight pass
Like vibrations of a bell,
And fashionable madmen raise
Their pedantic boring cry:
Every farthing of the cost,
All the dreaded cards foretell,
Shall be paid, but from this night
Not a whisper, not a thought,
Not a kiss nor look be lost.

Beauty, midnight, vision dies:
Let the winds of dawn that blow
Softly round your dreaming head
Such a day of sweetness show
Eye and knocking heart may bless,
Find the mortal world enough;
Noons of dryness see you fed
By the involuntary powers,
Nights of insult let you pass
Watched by every human love.

Danse Macabre

It's farewell to the drawing-room's civilised cry,
The professor's sensible whereto and why,
The frock-coated diplomat's social aplomb,
Now matters are settled with gas and with bomb.

The works for two pianos, the brilliant stories
Of reasonable giants and remarkable fairies,
The pictures, the ointments, the frangible wares
And the branches of olive are stored upstairs.

For the Devil has broken parole and arisen,
He has dynamited his way out of prison,
Out of the well where his Papa throws
The rebel angel, the outcast rose,

Like influenza he walks abroad,
He stands by the bridge, he waits by the ford,
As a goose or a gull he flies overhead,
He hides in the cupboard and under the bed.

Assuming such shapes as may best disguise
The hate that burns in his big blue eyes;
He may be a baby that croons in its pram,
Or a dear old grannie boarding a tram.

A plumber, a doctor, for he has skill
To adopt a serious profession at will;
Superb at ice-hockey, a prince at the dance,
He's fierce as the tigers, secretive as plants.

O were he to triumph, dear heart, you know
To what depths of shame he would drag you low;
He would steal you away from me, yes, my dear,
He would steal you and cut off your beautiful hair.

Millions already have come to their harm,
Succumbing like doves to his adder's charm;
Hundreds of trees in the wood are unsound:
I'm the axe that must cut them down to the ground.

For I, after all, am the Fortunate One,
The Happy-Go-Lucky, the spoilt Third Son;
For me it is written the Devil to chase
And to rid the earth of the human race.

The behaving of man is a world of horror,
A sedentary Sodom and slick Gomorrah;
I must take charge of the liquid fire
And storm the cities of human desire.

The buying and selling, the eating and drinking,
The disloyal machines and irreverent thinking,
The lovely dullards again and again
Inspiring their bitter ambitious men.

I shall come, I shall punish, the Devil be dead,
I shall have caviare thick on my bread,
I shall build myself a cathedral for home
With a vacuum cleaner in every room.

I shall ride the parade in a platinum car,
My features shall shine, my name shall be Star,
Day-long and night-long the bells I shall peal,
And down the long street I shall turn the cartwheel.

So Little John, Long John, Peter and Paul,
And poor little Horace with only one ball,
You shall leave your breakfast, your desk and your play
On a fine summer morning the Devil to slay.

For it's order and trumpet and anger and drum
And power and glory command you to come;
The graves shall fly open and let you all in,
And the earth shall be emptied of mortal sin.

The fishes are silent deep in the sea,
The skies are lit up like a Christmas tree,
The star in the West shoots its warning cry:
"Mankind is alive, but Mankind must die."

So good-bye to the house with its wallpaper red,
Good-bye to the sheets on the warm double bed,
Good-bye to the beautiful birds on the wall,
It's good-bye, dear heart, good-bye to you all.

Blues

(For Hedli Anderson)

Ladies and gentlemen, sitting here,
Eating and drinking and warming a chair,
Feeling and thinking and drawing your breath,
Who's sitting next to you? It may be Death.

As a high-stepping blondie with eyes of blue
In the subway, on beaches, Death looks at you;
And married or single or young or old,
You'll become a sugar daddy and do as you're told.

Death is a G-man. You may think yourself smart,
But he'll send you to the hot-seat or plug you through the heart;
He may be a slow worker, but in the end
He'll get you for the crime of being born, my friend.

Death as a doctor has first-class degrees;
The world is on his panel; he charges no fees;
He listens to your chest, says—"You're breathing. That's bad.
But don't worry; we'll soon see to that, my lad."

Death knocks at your door selling real estate,
The value of which will not depreciate;
It's easy, it's convenient, it's old world. You'll sign,
Whatever your income, on the dotted line.

Death as a teacher is simply grand;
The dumbest pupil can understand.
He has only one subject and that is the Tomb;
But no one ever yawns or asks to leave the room.

So whether you're standing broke in the rain,
Or playing poker or drinking champagne,
Death's looking for you, he's already on the way,
So look out for him to-morrow or perhaps to-day.

Give Up Love

Cleopatra, Anthony
Were introspective you'll agree,
Got in a morbid state because
They lounged about too much indoors.
If they'd gone in for Eton Fives
They wouldn't have gone and lost their lives.

For if you love sport then you won't give a thought
To all that goes on in the park.
Learning to bowl will keep your heart whole,
You won't want to go out after dark.
Love is unenglish and sloppy and soft
So be English and stringy and tough.
If you keep yourself fit you will never want It,
So give up Love.

Abelard and Heloise
Were a pair of sentimental geese.
They ought to have taken exercise,
Not spent their time in sighs and cries.
Gone in for netball or sailing boats
Instead of writing sloppy notes.

For if you can jump then you won't want to bump
By mistake into girls in the park.
If you can dive you won't yearn for High Life,
You won't want to go out after dark.
Love is unenglish and sloppy and soft
So be English and stringy and tough.
If you hole out in one, then love seems poor fun,
So give up Love.

Dante wrote a lot of slush
Because he got an unhealthy crush
On Beatrice who was dead to him.
He ought to have kept himself in trim
Upon the horizontal bars,
Not written tripe about the stars.

For if you keep a straight bat then love will seem flat
    It won't tempt you to spoon in the park
If your backhand's like this, then you won't want to kiss,
    You won't want to go out after dark.
Love is unenglish and sloppy and soft
    So be English and stringy and tough.
You won't feel the loss if you're good at lacrosse
    So give up Love.

Don Juan was another one
For whom something should have been done.
Compulsory games would have been the cure
For his nasty Spanish habits I'm sure.
Had someone seen that he played cricket
He would not have been so wicked.

For if you play games you will never write names
    On seats in the public park
Riding to hounds puts love out of bounds,
    You won't want to go out after dark
Love is unenglish and sloppy and soft
    So be English and stringy and tough.
Love makes you laugh if you play centre half
    So give up Love.

Nonsense Song

My love is like a red red rose
Or concerts for the blind,
She's like a mutton-chop before
And a rifle-range behind.

Her hair is like a looking-glass,
Her brow is like a bog,
Her eyes are like a flock of sheep
Seen through a London fog.

Her nose is like an Irish jig,
Her mouth is like a 'bus,
Her chin is like a bowl of soup
Shared between all of us.

Her form divine is like a map
Of the United States,
Her foot is like a motor-car
Without its number-plates.

No steeple-jack shall part us now
Nor fireman in a frock;
True love could sink a Channel boat
Or knit a baby's sock.

Johnny

O the valley in the summer where I and my John
Beside the deep river would walk on and on
While the flowers at our feet and the birds up above
Argued so sweetly on reciprocal love,
And I leaned on his shoulder; "O Johnny, let's play":
But he frowned like thunder and he went away.

O that Friday near Christmas as I well recall
When we went to the Charity Matinee Ball,
The floor was so smooth and the band was so loud
And Johnny so handsome I felt so proud;
"Squeeze me tighter, dear Johnny, let's dance till it's day":
But he frowned like thunder and he went away.

Shall I ever forget at the Grand Opera
When music poured out of each wonderful star?
Diamonds and pearls they hung dazzling down
Over each silver or golden silk gown;
"O John I'm in heaven", I whispered to say:
But he frowned like thunder and he went away.

O but he was as fair as a garden in flower,
As slender and tall as the great Eiffel Tower,
When the waltz throbbed out on the long promenade
O his eyes and his smile they went straight to my heart;
"O marry me, Johnny, I'll love and obey":
But he frowned like thunder and he went away.

O last night I dreamed of you, Johnny, my lover,
You'd the sun on one arm and the moon on the other,
The sea it was blue and the grass it was green,
Every star rattled a round tambourine;
Ten thousand miles deep in a pit there I lay:
But you frowned like thunder and you went away.

Miss Gee

Let me tell you a little story
    About Miss Edith Gee;
She lived in Clevedon Terrace
    At Number 83.

She'd a slight squint in her left eye,
    Her lips they were thin and small,
She had narrow sloping shoulders
    And she had no bust at all.

She'd a velvet hat with trimmings,
    And a dark-grey serge costume;
She lived in Clevedon Terrace
    In a small bed-sitting room.

She'd a purple mac for wet days,
    A green umbrella too to take,
She'd a bicycle with shopping basket
    And a harsh back-pedal brake.

The Church of Saint Aloysius
    Was not so very far;
She did a lot of knitting,
    Knitting for that Church Bazaar.

Miss Gee looked up at the starlight
    And said: "Does anyone care
That I live in Clevedon Terrace
    On one hundred pounds a year?"

She dreamed a dream one evening
    That she was the Queen of France
And the Vicar of Saint Aloysius
    Asked Her Majesty to dance.

But a storm blew down the palace,
    She was biking through a field of corn,
And a bull with the face of the Vicar
    Was charging with lowered horn.

She could feel his hot breath behind her,
    He was going to overtake;
And the bicycle went slower and slower
    Because of that back-pedal brake.

Summer made the trees a picture,
    Winter made them a wreck;
She bicycled to the evening service
    With her clothes buttoned up to her neck.

She passed by the loving couples,
    She turned her head away;
She passed by the loving couples
    And they didn't ask her to stay.

Miss Gee sat down in the side-aisle,
    She heard the organ play;
And the choir it sang so sweetly
    At the ending of the day.

Miss Gee knelt down in the side-aisle,
    She knelt down on her knees;
"Lead me not into temptation
    But make me a good girl, please."

The days and nights went by her
    Like waves round a Cornish wreck;
She bicycled down to the doctor
    With her clothes buttoned up to her neck.

She bicycled down to the doctor,
    And rang the surgery bell;
"O, doctor, I've a pain inside me,
    And I don't feel very well."

Doctor Thomas looked her over,
    And then he looked some more;
Walked over to his wash-basin,
    Said: "Why didn't you come before?"

Doctor Thomas sat over his dinner,
    Though his wife was waiting to ring;
Rolling his bread into pellets,
    Said: "Cancer's a funny thing.

"Nobody knows what the cause is,
    Though some pretend they do;
It's like some hidden assassin
    Waiting to strike at you.

"Childless women get it,
    And men when they retire;
It's as if there had to be some outlet
    For their foiled creative fire."

His wife she rang for the servant,
    Said: "Don't be so morbid, dear";
He said: "I saw Miss Gee this evening
    And she's a goner, I fear."

They took Miss Gee to the hospital,
    She lay there a total wreck,
Lay in the ward for women
    With the bedclothes right up to her neck.

They laid her on the table,
    The students began to laugh;
And Mr Rose the surgeon
    He cut Miss Gee in half.

Mr Rose he turned to his students,
    Said: "Gentlemen, if you please,
We seldom see a sarcoma
    As far advanced as this."

They took her off the table,
    They wheeled away Miss Gee
Down to another department
    Where they study Anatomy.

They hung her from the ceiling,
    Yes, they hung up Miss Gee;
And a couple of Oxford Groupers
    Carefully dissected her knee.

Victor

Victor was a little baby,
        Into this world he came;
His father took him on his knee and said:
        "Don't dishonour the family name."

Victor looked up at his father
        Looked up with big round eyes;
His father said: "Victor, my only son,
        Don't you ever ever tell lies."

Victor and his father went riding
        Out in a little dog-cart;
His father took a Bible from his pocket and read:
        "Blessed are the pure in heart."

It was a frosty December,
        It wasn't the season for fruits;
His father fell dead of heart disease
        While lacing up his boots.

It was a frosty December
        When into his grave he sank;
His uncle found Victor a post as cashier
        In the Midland Counties Bank.

It was a frosty December
        Victor was only eighteen,
But his figures were neat and his margins straight
        And his cuffs were always clean.

He took a room at the Peveril,
        A respectable boarding-house;
And Time watched Victor day after day
        As a cat will watch a mouse.

The clerks slapped Victor on the shoulder;
  "Have you ever had a woman?" they said,
"Come down town with us on Saturday night."
  Victor smiled and shook his head.

The manager sat in his office,
  Smoked a Corona cigar;
Said: "Victor's a decent fellow but
  He's too mousey to go far."

Victor went up to his bedroom,
  Set the alarum bell;
Climbed into bed, took his Bible and read
  Of what happened to Jezebel.

It was the First of April,
  Anna to the Peveril came;
Her eyes, her lips, her breasts, her hips
  And her smile set men aflame.

She looked as pure as a schoolgirl
  On her First Communion day,
But her kisses were like the best champagne
  When she gave herself away.

It was the Second of April,
  She was wearing a coat of fur;
Victor met her upon the stairs
  And he fell in love with her.

The first time he made his proposal,
  She laughed, said: "I'll never wed";
The second time there was a pause,
  Then she smiled and shook her head.

Anna looked into her mirror,
  Pouted and gave a frown;
Said: "Victor's as dull as a wet afternoon
  But I've got to settle down."

The third time he made his proposal,
          As they walked by the Reservoir,
She gave him a kiss like a blow on the head,
          Said: "You are my heart's desire."

They were married early in August,
          She said: "Kiss me, you funny boy";
Victor took her in his arms and said:
          "O my Helen of Troy."

It was the middle of September,
          Victor came to the office one day;
He was wearing a flower in his buttonhole,
          He was late but he was gay.

The clerks were talking of Anna,
          The door was just ajar;
One said: "Poor old Victor, but where ignorance
          Is bliss, etcetera."

Victor stood still as a statue,
          The door was just ajar;
One said: "God, what fun I had with her
          In that Baby Austin car."

Victor walked out into the High Street,
          He walked to the edge of the town;
He came to the allotments and the rubbish heaps
          And his tears came tumbling down.

Victor looked up at the sunset
          As he stood there all alone;
Cried: "Are you in Heaven, Father?"
          But the sky said "Address not known."

Victor looked up at the mountains,
          The mountains all covered with snow;
Cried: "Are you pleased with me, Father?"
          And the answer came back, "No."

Victor came to the forest,
Cried: "Father, will she ever be true?"
And the oaks and the beeches shook their heads
And they answered: "Not to you."

Victor came to the meadow
Where the wind went sweeping by;
Cried: "O Father, I love her so,"
But the wind said: "She must die."

Victor came to the river
Running so deep and so still;
Crying: "O Father, what shall I do?"
And the river answered: "Kill."

Anna was sitting at table,
Drawing cards from a pack;
Anna was sitting at table
Waiting for her husband to come back.

It wasn't the Jack of Diamonds
Nor the Joker she drew at first;
It wasn't the King or the Queen of Hearts
But the Ace of Spades reversed.

Victor stood in the doorway,
He didn't utter a word;
She said: "What's the matter, darling?"
He behaved as if he hadn't heard.

There was a voice in his left ear,
There was a voice in his right,
There was a voice at the base of his skull
Saying: "She must die to-night."

Victor picked up a carving-knife,
His features were set and drawn,
Said: "Anna, it would have been better for you
If you had not been born."

Anna jumped up from the table,
     Anna started to scream,
But Victor came slowly after her
     Like a horror in a dream.

She dodged behind the sofa,
     She tore down a curtain rod,
But Victor came slowly after her,
     Said: "Prepare to meet Thy God."

She managed to wrench the door open,
     She ran and she didn't stop.
But Victor followed her up the stairs
     And he caught her at the top.

He stood there above the body,
     He stood there holding the knife;
And the blood ran down the stairs and sang:
     "I'm the Resurrection and the Life."

They tapped Victor on the shoulder,
     They took him away in a van;
He sat as quiet as a lump of moss
     Saying: "I am the Son of Man."

Victor sat in a corner
     Making a woman of clay,
Saying: "I am Alpha and Omega, I shall come
     To judge the earth one day."

James Honeyman

James Honeyman was a silent child
He didn't laugh or cry;
He looked at his mother
With curiosity.

Mother came up to the nursery,
Peeped through the open door,
Saw him striking matches
Sitting on the nursery floor.

He went to the children's party,
The buns were full of cream;
Sat dissolving sugar
In his teacup in a dream.

On his eighth birthday
Didn't care that the day was wet
For by his bedside
Lay a ten-shilling chemistry set.

Teacher said: "James Honeyman's
The cleverest boy we've had,
But he doesn't play with the others
And that, I think, is sad."

While the other boys played football
He worked in the laboratory
Got a scholarship to college,
And a first-class degree.

Kept awake with black coffee,
Took to wearing glasses,
Writing a thesis
On the toxic gases.

Went out into the country,
Went by a Green Line Bus,
Walked on the Chilterns,
Thought about Phosphorus.

Said: "Lewisite in its day
Was pretty decent stuff,
But under modern conditions
It's not nearly strong enough."

His Tutor sipped his port,
Said: "I think it's clear
That young James Honeyman's
The most brilliant man of his year."

He got a job in research
With Imperial Alkali,
Said to himself while shaving:
"I'll be famous before I die."

His landlady said: "Mr Honeyman,
You've only got one life,
You ought to have some fun, Sir.
You ought to find a wife."

At Imperial Alkali
There was a girl called Doreen,
One day she cut her finger,
Asked him for iodine.

"I'm feeling faint", she said.
He led her to a chair,
Fetched her a glass of water,
Wanted to stroke her hair.

They took a villa on the Great West Road,
Painted green and white;
On their left a United Dairy,
A cinema on their right.

At the bottom of his garden
He built a little shed.
"He's going to blow us up",
All the neighbours said.

Doreen called down at midnight:
"Jim dear, it's time for bed."
"I'll finish my experiment
And then I'll come", he said.

Caught influenza at Christmas,
The Doctor said: "Go to bed."
"I'll finish my experiment
And then I'll go", he said.

Walked out on Sundays,
Helped to push the pram,
Said: "I'm looking for a gas, dear;
A whiff will kill a man."

"I'm going to find it,
That's what I'm going to do."
Doreen squeezed his hand and said:
"Jim, I believe in you."

In the hot nights of summer
When the roses all were red
James Honeyman was working
In his little garden shed.

Came upstairs at midnight,
Kissed his sleeping son,
Held up a sealed glass test-tube,
Said: "Look, Doreen, I've won!"

They stood together by the window,
The moon was bright and clear.
He said: "At last I've done something
That's worthy of you, dear."

Took a train next morning,
Went up to Whitehall
With the phial in his pocket
To show it to them all.

Sent in his card,
The officials only swore:
"Tell him we're very busy
And show him the door."

Doreen said to the neighbours:
"Isn't it a shame?
My husband's so clever
And they didn't know his name."

One neighbour was sympathetic,
Her name was Mrs Flower.
She was the agent
Of a foreign power.

One evening they sat at supper,
There came a gentle knock:
"A gentleman to see Mr Honeyman."
He stayed till eleven o'clock.

They walked down the garden together,
Down to the little shed:
"We'll see you, then, in Paris.
Good night", the gentleman said.

The boat was nearing Dover,
He looked back at Calais:
Said: "Honeyman's N.P.C.
Will be heard of, some day."

He was sitting in the garden
Writing notes on a pad,
Their little son was playing
Round his mother and dad.

Suddenly from the east
Some aeroplanes appeared,
Somebody screamed: "They're bombers!
War must have been declared!"

The first bomb hit the Dairy,
The second the cinema,
The third fell in the garden
Just like a falling star.

"Oh kiss me, Mother, kiss me,
And tuck me up in bed
For Daddy's invention
Is going to choke me dead!"

"Where are you, James, where are you?
Oh put your arms round me,
For my lungs are full
Of Honeyman's N.P.C.!"

"I wish I were a salmon
Swimming in the sea,
I wish I were the dove
That coos upon the tree."

"Oh you are not a salmon,
Oh you are not a dove;
But you invented the vapour
That is killing those you love."

"Oh hide me in the mountains,
Oh drown me in the sea.
Lock me in the dungeon
And throw away the key."

"Oh you can't hide in the mountains,
Oh you can't drown in the sea,
But you must die, and you know why,
By Honeyman's N.P.C.!"

Roman Wall Blues

Over the heather the wet wind blows,
I've lice in my tunic and a cold in my nose.

The rain comes pattering out of the sky,
I'm a Wall soldier, I don't know why.

The mist creeps over the hard grey stone,
My girl's in Tungria; I sleep alone.

Aulus goes hanging around her place,
I don't like his manners, I don't like his face.

Piso's a Christian, he worships a fish;
There'd be no kissing if he had his wish.

She gave me a ring but I diced it away;
I want my girl and I want my pay.

When I'm a veteran with only one eye
I shall do nothing but look at the sky.

As I Walked Out One Evening

As I walked out one evening,
    Walking down Bristol Street,
The crowds upon the pavement
    Were fields of harvest wheat.

And down by the brimming river
    I heard a lover sing
Under an arch of the railway:
    "Love has no ending.

"I'll love you, dear, I'll love you
    Till China and Africa meet
And the river jumps over the mountain
    And the salmon sing in the street.

"I'll love you till the ocean
    Is folded and hung up to dry
And the seven stars go squawking
    Like geese about the sky.

"The years shall run like rabbits
    For in my arms I hold
The Flower of the Ages
    And the first love of the world."

But all the clocks in the city
    Began to whirr and chime:
"O let not Time deceive you,
    You cannot conquer Time.

"In the burrows of the Nightmare
    Where Justice naked is,
Time watches from the shadow
    And coughs when you would kiss.

"In headaches and in worry
 Vaguely life leaks away,
And Time will have his fancy
 To-morrow or to-day.

"Into many a green valley
 Drifts the appalling snow;
Time breaks the threaded dances
 And the diver's brilliant bow.

"O plunge your hands in water,
 Plunge them in up to the wrist;
Stare, stare in the basin
 And wonder what you've missed.

"The glacier knocks in the cupboard,
 The desert sighs in the bed,
And the crack in the tea-cup opens
 A lane to the land of the dead.

"Where the beggars raffle the banknotes
 And the Giant is enchanting to Jack,
And the Lily-white Boy is a Roarer
 And Jill goes down on her back.

"O look, look in the mirror,
 O look in your distress;
Life remains a blessing
 Although you cannot bless.

"O stand, stand at the window
 As the tears scald and start;
You shall love your crooked neighbour
 With your crooked heart."

It was late, late in the evening,
 The lovers they were gone;
The clocks had ceased their chiming
 And the deep river ran on.

O Tell Me the Truth About Love

Some say that Love's a little boy
       And some say he's a bird,
Some say he makes the world go round
       And some say that's absurd:
But when I asked the man next door
       Who looked as if he knew,
His wife was very cross indeed
       And said it wouldn't do.

Does it look like a pair of pyjamas
       Or the ham in a temperance hotel,
Does its odour remind one of llamas
       Or has it a comforting smell?
Is it prickly to touch as a hedge is
       Or soft as eiderdown fluff,
Is it sharp or quite smooth at the edges?
       O tell me the truth about love.

The history books refer to it
       In cryptic little notes,
And it's a common topic on
       The Trans-Atlantic boats;
I've found the subject mentioned in
       Accounts of suicides,
And even seen it scribbled on
       The backs of railway guides.

Does it howl like a hungry Alsatian
       Or boom like a military band,
Could one give a first-class imitation
       On a saw or a Steinway Grand,
Is its singing at parties a riot,
       Does it only like Classical stuff,
Will it stop when one wants to be quiet?
       O tell me the truth about love.

I looked inside the summer-house,
       It wasn't ever there,
I've tried the Thames at Maidenhead
       And Brighton's bracing air;
I don't know what the blackbird sang
       Or what the roses said,
But it wasn't in the chicken-run
       Or underneath the bed.

Can it pull extraordinary faces,
       Is it usually sick on a swing,
Does it spend all its time at the races
       Or fiddling with pieces of string,
Has it views of its own about money,
       Does it think Patriotism enough,
Are its stories vulgar but funny?
       O tell me the truth about love.

Your feelings when you meet it, I
       Am told you can't forget,
I've sought it since I was a child
       But haven't found it yet;
I'm getting on for thirty-five,
       And still I do not know
What kind of creature it can be
       That bothers people so.

When it comes, will it come without warning
       Just as I'm picking my nose,
Will it knock on my door in the morning
       Or tread in the bus on my toes,
Will it come like a change in the weather,
       Will its greeting be courteous or bluff,
Will it alter my life altogether?
       O tell me the truth about love.

Gare du Midi

A nondescript express in from the South,
Crowds round the ticket barrier, a face
To welcome which the mayor has not contrived
Bugles or braid: something about the mouth
Distracts the stray look with alarm and pity.
Snow is falling. Clutching a little case,
He walks out briskly to infect a city
Whose terrible future may have just arrived.

Epitaph on a Tyrant

Perfection, of a kind, was what he was after,
And the poetry he invented was easy to understand;
He knew human folly like the back of his hand,
And was greatly interested in armies and fleets;
When he laughed, respectable senators burst with laughter,
And when he cried the little children died in the streets.

The Unknown Citizen

He was found by the Bureau of Statistics to be
One against whom there was no official complaint,
And all the reports on his conduct agree
That, in the modern sense of an old-fashioned word, he was a saint,
For in everything he did he served the Greater Community.
Except for the War till the day he retired
He worked in a factory and never got fired,
But satisfied his employers, Fudge Motors Inc.
Yet he wasn't a scab or odd in his views,
For his Union reports that he paid his dues,
(Our report on his Union shows it was sound)
And our Social Psychology workers found
That he was popular with his mates and liked a drink.
The Press are convinced that he bought a paper every day
And that his reactions to advertisements were normal in every way.
Policies taken out in his name prove that he was fully insured,
And his Health-card shows he was once in hospital but left it cured.
Both Producers Research and High-Grade Living declare
He was fully sensible to the advantages of the Installment Plan
And had everything necessary to the Modern Man,
A gramophone, a radio, a car and a frigidaire.
Our researchers into Public Opinion are content
That he held the proper opinions for the time of year;
When there was peace, he was for peace; when there was
                                    war, he went.
He was married and added five children to the population,
Which our Eugenist says was the right number for a parent of his
                                    generation,
And our teachers report that he never interfered with their education.
Was he free? Was he happy? The question is absurd:
Had anything been wrong, we should certainly have heard.

Refugee Blues

Say this city has ten million souls,
Some are living in mansions, some are living in holes:
Yet there's no place for us, my dear, yet there's no place for us.

Once we had a country and we thought it fair,
Look in the atlas and you'll find it there:
We cannot go there now, my dear, we cannot go there now.

In the village churchyard there grows an old yew,
Every spring it blossoms anew:
Old passports can't do that, my dear, old passports can't do that.

The consul banged the table and said;
"If you've got no passport you're officially dead:"
But we are still alive, my dear, but we are still alive.

Went to a committee; they offered me a chair;
Asked me politely to return next year:
But where shall we go to-day, my dear, but where shall we go
                                                    to-day?

Came to a public meeting; the speaker got up and said;
"If we let them in, they will steal our daily bread":
He was talking of you and me, my dear, he was talking of you
                                                    and me.

Thought I heard the thunder rumbling in the sky;
It was Hitler over Europe, saying; "They must die":
O we were in his mind, my dear, O we were in his mind.

Saw a poodle in a jacket fastened with a pin,
Saw a door opened and a cat let in:
But they weren't German Jews, my dear, but they weren't German
                                                    Jews.

Went down the harbour and stood upon the quay,
Saw the fish swimming as if they were free:
Only ten feet away, my dear, only ten feet away.

Walked through a wood, saw the birds in the trees;
They had no politicians and sang at their ease:
They weren't the human race, my dear, they weren't the human race.

Dreamed I saw a building with a thousand floors,
A thousand windows and a thousand doors:
Not one of them was ours, my dear, not one of them was ours.

Stood on a great plain in the falling snow;
Ten thousand soldiers marched to and fro:
Looking for you and me, my dear, looking for you and me.

Ode

In this epoch of high-pressure selling
    When the salesman gives us no rest,
And even Governments are yelling
    "Our Brand is Better than Best";
When the hoardings announce a new diet
    To take all our odor away,
Or a medicine to keep the kids quiet,
    Or a belt that will give us S.A.,
Or a soap to wash shirts in a minute,
    One wonders at times, I'm afraid,
If there is one word of truth in it,
    And how much the writers were paid.

O is there a technique to praise the
    HOTEL GEORGE WASHINGTON then,
That doesn't resemble the ways the
    Really professional men
Convince a two-hundred-pound matron
    She's the feather she was in her youth?
Well, considering who is the patron,
    I think I shall stick to the truth.
It stands on the Isle of Manhattan,
    Not far from the Lexington line,
And although it's démodé to fatten,
    There's a ballroom where parties may dine.

The walls look unlikely to crumble
    And although, to be perfectly fair,
A few entomologists grumble
    That bugs are exceedingly rare,
The Normal Man life is so rich in
    Will not be disgusted, perhaps,
To learn that there's food in the kitchen,
    And that water comes out of the taps,

That the sheets are not covered with toffee,
    And I think he may safely assume
That he won't find a fish in his coffee
    Or a very large snake in his room.

While the curious student may study
    All the sorts and conditions of men,
And distinguish the Bore from the Buddy,
    And the Fowl from the Broody Old Hen;
And presently learn to discover
    How one looks when one's deeply in debt,
And which one is in search of a lover,
    And which one is in need of a vet;
And among all these Mrs and Mr's,
    To detect as each couple arrives,
How many are really their sisters,
    And how many are simply their wives.

But now let me add in conclusion
    Just one little personal remark;
Though I know that the Self's an illusion,
    And that words leave us all in the dark,
That we're serious mental cases
    If we think that we think that we know,
Yet I've stayed in hotels in most places
    Where my passport permits me to go
(Excluding the British Dominions
    And Turkey and U.S.S.R.)
And this one, in my humble opinion's
    The nicest I've been in so far.

Calypso

Driver drive faster and make a good run
Down the Springfield Line under the shining sun.

Fly like the aeroplane, don't pull up short
Till you brake for Grand Central Station, New York.

For there in the middle of that waiting hall
Should be standing the one that I love best of all.

If he's not there to meet me when I get to town,
I'll stand on the pavement with tears rolling down.

For he is the one that I love to look on,
The acme of kindness and perfection.

He presses my hand and he says he loves me
Which I find an admirable peculiarity.

The woods are bright green on both sides of the line;
The trees have their loves though they're different from mine.

But the poor fat old banker in the sun-parlour car
Has no one to love him except his cigar.

If I were the head of the Church or the State
I'd powder my nose and just tell them to wait.

For love's more important and powerful than
Even a priest or a politician.

Heavy Date

Sharp and silent in the
Clear October lighting
Of a Sunday morning
    The great city lies;
And I at a window
Looking over water
At the world of Business
    With a lover's eyes.

All mankind, I fancy,
When anticipating
Anything exciting
    Like a rendez-vous,
Occupy the time in
Purely random thinking,
For when love is waiting
    Logic will not do.

Much as he would like to
Concentrate completely
On the precious Object,
    Love has not the power:
Goethe put it neatly;
No one cares to watch the
Loveliest sunset after
    Quarter of an hour.

So I pass the time, dear,
Till I see you, writing
Down whatever nonsense
    Comes into my head;
Let the life that has been
Lightly buried in my
Personal Unconscious
    Rise up from the dead.

Why association
Should see fit to set a
Bull-dog by a trombone
          On a grassy plain
Littered with old letters,
Leaves me simply guessing,
I suppose it's La Con-
          -dition Humaine.

As at lantern lectures
Image follows image;
Here comes a steam-roller
          Through an orange grove,
Driven by a nursemaid
As she sadly mutters:
"Zola, poor old Zola
          Murdered by a stove."

Now I hear Saint Francis
Telling me in breezy
Tones as we are walking
          Near a power-house:
"Loving birds is easy,
Any fool can do it,
But I must admit it's
          Hard to love the louse."

Malinowski, Rivers,
Benedict and others
Show how common culture
          Shapes the separate lives:
Matrilineal races
Kill their mothers' brothers
In their dreams and turn their
          Sisters into wives.

As an intellectual
Member of the Middle
Classes or what-have-you
        So I have to dream:
Essence without Form is
Free but ineffectual,
Birth and education
        Guide the living stream.

Who when looking over
Faces in the subway,
Each with its uniqueness,
        Would not, did he dare,
Ask what forms exactly
Suited to their weakness
Love and desperation
        Take to govern there.

Would not like to know what
Influence occupation
Has on human vision
        Of the human fate:
Do all clerks for instance
Pigeon-hole creation,
Brokers see the Ding-an-
        -sich as Real Estate?

When a politician
Dreams about his sweetheart,
Does he multiply her
        Face into a crowd,
Are her fond responses
All-or-none reactions,
Does he try to buy her,
        Is the kissing loud?

Strange are love's mutations:
Thus, the early poem
Of the flesh sub rosa
          Has been known to grow
Now and then into the
Amor intellectu-
-alis of Spinoza;
          How we do not know.

Slowly we are learning,
We at least know this much,
That we have to unlearn
          Much that we were taught,
And are growing chary
Of emphatic dogmas;
Love like Matter is much
          Odder than we thought.

Love requires an Object,
But this varies so much,
Almost, I imagine,
          Anything will do:
When I was a child, I
Loved a pumping-engine,
Thought it every bit as
          Beautiful as you.

Love has no position,
Love's a way of living,
One kind of relation
          Possible between
Any things or persons
Given one condition,
The one sine qua non
          Being mutual need.

Through it we discover
An essential secret
Called by some Salvation
        And by some Success;
Crying for the moon is
Naughtiness and envy,
We can only love what-
        -ever we possess.

I believed for years that
Love was the conjunction
Of two oppositions;
        That was all untrue;
Every young man fears that
He is not worth loving:
Bless you, darling, I have
        Found myself in you.

I should love to go on
Telling how I love you,
Thanking you for happy
        Changes in my life,
But it would be silly
Seeing that you know it
And that any moment
        Now you may arrive.

When two lovers meet, then
There's an end of writing
Thought and Analytics:
        Lovers, like the dead,
In their loves are equal;
Sophomores and peasants,
Poets and their critics
        Are the same in bed.

Song

Warm are the still and lucky miles,
White shores of longing stretch away,
The light of recognition fills
    The whole great day, and bright
The tiny world of lovers' arms.

Silence invades the breathing wood
Where drowsy limbs a treasure keep,
Now greenly falls the learned shade
    Across the sleeping brows
And stirs their secret to a smile.

Restored! Returned! The lost are born
On seas of shipwreck home at last:
See! In the fire of praising burns
    The dry dumb past, and we
The life–day long shall part no more.

"Gold in the North" Came the Blizzard to Say

"Gold in the North," came the blizzard to say,
I left my sweetheart at the break of day,
The gold ran out and my love turned grey.
You don't know all, sir, you don't know all.

"The West," said the sun, "for enterprise,"
A bullet in Frisco put me wise,
My last words were "God damn your eyes."
You don't know all, sir, you don't know all.

In the streets of New York I was young and swell,
I rode the market, the market fell,
One morning I woke and found myself in hell,
You don't know all, sir, you don't know all.

In Alabama my heart was full,
Down by the river bank I stole,
The waters of grief went over my soul,
You don't know all, ma'am, you don't know all.

In the saloons I heaved a sigh,
Lost in deserts of alkali I lay down to die;
There's always a sorrow can get you down,
All the world's whiskey won't ever drown.

Some think they're strong, some think they're smart,
Like butterflies they're pulled apart,
America can break your heart.
You don't know all, sir, you don't know all.

The Glamour Boys and Girls
Have Grievances Too

Chorus of Film Stars
and Models.

You've no idea how dull it is
Just being perfect nullities,
    The idols of a democratic nation,
The heroes of the multitude,
Their dreams of female pulchritude;
    We're very, very tired of admiration.

Woman Film Star.
Man Film Star.
Both.

My measurement around the hips,
The cut of my mustache and lips,
    Obey the whims of fashion;
In our embraces we select
Whatever technique seems correct
To give the visual effect
    Of an Eternal Passion.

Female Models.

On beaches or in night clubs I
Excel at femininity.

Male Models.

    And I at all athletics;
I pay attention to my hair.

Female Models.
Male Models.
Female Models.

For personal hygiene I've a flair,
The Hercules of underwear,
    The Venus of cosmetics.

Chorus.

We're bored with being glamorous,
We're bored with being amorous,
    For all our fans we don't give a banana;
Who wants to be exhibited
To all the world's inhibited
    As representative Americana?

Women Film Stars.　　The things a man of eighty-two
　　　　　　　　　　Will ask of his dream ingénue
　　　　　　　　　　　　　I shouldn't like to retail.
　　　　　　　　　　Unless you've tried to play Mamma,
　　　　　　　　　　You can't guess how particular
　　　　　　　　　　Young men who miss their mothers are
　　　　　　　　　　　　　About each little detail.

Men Film Stars.　　Rescuing girls from waterfalls,
　　　　　　　　　　Or shooting up the sheriff, palls
　　　　　　　　　　　　　Like any violent action.
　　　　　　　　　　We never want to die again,
　　　　　　　　　　Or throw a custard pie again,
　　　　　　　　　　To give the decent citizen
　　　　　　　　　　　　　Vicarious satisfaction.

Quartet of Film Stars.　The growth of social consciousness
　　　　　　　　　　Has failed to make our problems less,
　　　　　　　　　　　　　Indeed, they grow intenser:
　　　　　　　　　　And what with Freud and what with Marx,
　　　　　　　　　　With bureaucrats and matriarchs,
　　　　　　　　　　The chances are our little larks
　　　　　　　　　　　　　Will not get past the censor.

　　　　　　　　　　You'd hate it if you were employed
　　　　　　　　　　To be a sin in celluloid
　　　　　　　　　　　　　Or else a saint in plaster;
　　　　　　　　　　O little hearts who make a fuss,
　　　　　　　　　　What pleasure it would be to us
　　　　　　　　　　To give the bird to Oedipus,
　　　　　　　　　　　　　The raspberry to Jocasta.

Chorus.　　　　　You've no idea how dull it is
　　　　　　　　　　Just being perfect nullities,
　　　　　　　　　　　　　The idols of a democratic nation,
　　　　　　　　　　The heroes of the multitude,
　　　　　　　　　　Their dreams of female pulchritude;
　　　　　　　　　　　　　We're VERY, VERY tired of admiration.

Carry Her Over the Water

Carry her over the water,
        And set her down under the tree,
Where the culvers white all day and all night,
        And the winds from every quarter
Sing agreeably, agreeably, agreeably of love.

Put a gold ring on her finger,
        And press her close to your heart,
While the fish in the lake their snapshots take,
        And the frog, that sanguine singer,
Sings agreeably, agreeably, agreeably of love.

The streets shall all flock to your marriage,
        The houses turn round to look,
The tables and chairs say suitable prayers,
        And the horses drawing your carriage
Sing agreeably, agreeably, agreeably of love.

Eyes Look into the Well

Eyes look into the well,
Tears run down from the eye;
The tower cracked and fell
From the quiet winter sky.

Under the midnight stone
Love was buried by thieves;
The robbed heart begs for a bone,
The damned rustle like leaves.

Face down in the flooded brook
With nothing more to say,
Lies One the soldiers took,
And spoiled and threw away.

Lady Weeping at the Crossroads

Lady, weeping at the crossroads
Would you meet your love
In the twilight with his greyhounds,
And the hawk on his glove?

Bribe the birds then on the branches,
Bribe them to be dumb,
Stare the hot sun out of heaven
That the night may come.

Starless are the nights of travel,
Bleak the winter wind;
Run with terror all before you
And regret behind.

Run until you hear the ocean's
Everlasting cry;
Deep though it may be and bitter
You must drink it dry.

Wear out patience in the lowest
Dungeons of the sea,
Searching through the stranded shipwrecks
For the golden key.

Push onto the world's end, pay the
Dread guard with a kiss;
Cross the rotten bridge that totters
Over the abyss.

There stands the deserted castle
Ready to explore;
Enter, climb the marble staircase
Open the locked door.

Cross the silent empty ballroom,
Doubt and danger past;
Blow the cobwebs from the mirror
See yourself at last.

Put your hand behind the wainscot,
You have done your part;
Find the penknife there and plunge it
Into your false heart.

Notes

Parents once upon a time
Thought that acting was a crime;
"Daughter," many of them said,
"We would rather see you dead
Than upon a public stage."
Ours is a more liberal age:
Not a father breaks his heart
If she does Commercial Art,
Not a mother's hair turns grey
If her only son to-day
Find an outlet of expression
In the journalist profession.

. . .

His ageing nature is the same
As when childhood wore its name
In an atmosphere of love
And to itself appeared enough:
Only now when he has come
In walking distance of his tomb,
He at last discovers who
He had always been to whom
He so often was untrue.

. . .

Infants in their mothers' arms
Exercise their budding charms
On their fingers and their toes,
Striving ever to enclose
In the circle of their will
Objects disobedient still.
But the boy comes soon enough
To the limits of self-love,
And the adult learns how small
Is the individual,
How much stronger is the state
That will not co-operate
With the kingdom of his mind:
All his lifetime he will find
Swollen knee or aching tooth
Hostile to his search for truth;
Never will his sex belong
To his world of right and wrong,
Its libido comprehend
Who is foe and who is friend.

. . .

Do we want to return to the womb? Not at all.
No one really desires the impossible.
That is only the image out of our past
We practical people use when we cast
Our eyes on the future, to whom freedom is
The absence of all dualities.
Since there never can be much of that for us
In the universe of Copernicus,
Any heaven we think it decent to enter
Must be Ptolemaic with ourselves at the centre.

. . .

Base words are uttered only by the base
And can, as such, be clearly understood:
But noble platitudes—ah, there's a case
When the most careful scrutiny is needed
To tell the orator who's really good
From one who's base but merely has succeeded.

. . .

Once for candy cook had stolen
X was punished by Papa;
When he asked where babies came from
He was lied to by Mama.

Now the city streets are waiting
To mislead him, and he must
Keep an eye on aged beggars
Lest they strike him in disgust.

. . .

The Champion smiles—What Personality!
The Challenger scowls—How horrid he must be!
But let the Belt change hands and they change places—
Still from the same old corners come the same grimaces.

. . .

These public men who seem so to enjoy their dominion,
With their ruined faces and their voices treble with hate,
Are no less martyred because unaware of their fetters:
What would *you* be like were you never allowed to create
Or reflect, but compelled to give an immediate opinion,
Condemned to destroy or distribute the works of your betters?

.   .   .

Hans-in-Kelder, Hans-in-Kelder,
    What are you waiting for?
We need your strong arm to look after the farm
    And keep the wolf from the door.

Hans-in-Kelder, Hans-in-Kelder,
    Came out of the parsley-bed,
Came out at a run and leveled a gun
    And shot his old parents dead.

.   .   .

With what conviction the young man spoke
When he thought his nonsense rather a joke:
Now, when he doesn't doubt any more,
No one believes the booming old bore.

.   .   .

When statesmen gravely say—"We must be realistic—"
The chances are they're weak and therefore pacifistic:
But when they speak of Principles—look out—perhaps
Their generals are already poring over maps.

.   .   .

—"Don't you dream of a world, a society with no coercion?"
—"Yes, where a foetus is able to refuse to be born."

. . .

Only God can tell the saintly from the suburban,
Counterfeit virtues always resemble the true;
Neither in Life nor Art is honesty bohemian,
The free behave much as the respectable do.

. . .

To the man-in-the-street, who, I'm sorry to say,
    Is a keen observer of life,
The word Intellectual suggests straight away
    A man who's untrue to his wife.

. . .

What will cure the nation's ill?
A leader with a selfless will.
But how can you find this leader of yours?
By a process of Natural Selection of course.

The Way

Fresh addenda are published every day
To the encyclopedia of the Way.

Linguistic notes and scientific explanations,
And texts for schools with modernized spelling and illustrations.

Now everyone knows the hero must choose the old horse,
Abstain from liquor and sexual intercourse

And look out for a stranded fish to be kind to:
Now everyone thinks he could find, had he a mind to,

The way through the waste to the chapel in the rock
For a vision of the Triple Rainbow or the Astral Clock.

Forgetting his information comes mostly from married men
Who liked fishing and a flutter on the horses now and then.

And how reliable can any truth be that is got
By observing oneself and then just inserting a Not?

Song for St Cecilia's Day

I

In a garden shady this holy lady
With reverent cadence and subtle psalm,
Like a black swan as death came on
Poured forth her song in perfect calm:
And by ocean's margin this innocent virgin
Constructed an organ to enlarge her prayer,
And notes tremendous from her great engine
Thundered out on the Roman air.

Blonde Aphrodite rose up excited,
Moved to delight by the melody,
White as an orchid she rode quite naked
In an oyster shell on top of the sea;
At sounds so entrancing the angels dancing
Came out of their trance into time again,
And around the wicked in Hell's abysses
The huge flame flickered and eased their pain.

Blessed Cecilia, appear in visions
To all musicians, appear and inspire:
Translated Daughter, come down and startle
Composing mortals with immortal fire.

II

I cannot grow;
I have no shadow
To run away from,
I only play.

I cannot err;
There is no creature
Whom I belong to,
Whom I could wrong.

I am defeat
When it knows it
Can now do nothing
By suffering.

All you lived through,
Dancing because you
No longer need it
For any deed.

I shall never be
Different. Love me.

III

O ear whose creatures cannot wish to fall,
O calm of spaces unafraid of weight,
Where Sorrow is herself, forgetting all
The gaucheness of her adolescent state,
Where Hope within the altogether strange
From every outworn image is released,
And Dread born whole and normal like a beast
Into a world of truths that never change:
Restore our fallen day; O re-arrange.

O dear white children casual as birds,
Playing among the ruined languages,
So small beside their large confusing words,
So gay against the greater silences
Of dreadful things you did: O hang the head,
Impetuous child with the tremendous brain,
O weep, child, weep, O weep away the stain,
Lost innocence who wished your lover dead,
Weep for the lives your wishes never led.

O cry created as the bow of sin
Is drawn across our trembling violin.
O weep, child, weep, O weep away the stain.
O law drummed out by hearts against the still
Long winter of our intellectual will.
That what has been may never be again.
O flute that throbs with the thanksgiving breath
Of convalescents on the shores of death.
O bless the freedom that you never chose.
O trumpets that unguarded children blow
About the fortress of their inner foe.
O wear your tribulation like a rose.

Many Happy Returns

(For John Rettger)

Johnny, since today is
February the twelfth when
Neighbours and relations
    Think of you and wish,
Though a staunch Aquarian,
Graciously accept the
Verbal celebrations
    Of a doubtful Fish.

Seven years ago you
Warmed your mother's heart by
Making a successful
    Début on our stage;
Naiveté's an act that
You already know you
Cannot get away with
    Even at your age.

So I wish you first a
Sense of theatre; only
Those who love illusion
    And know it will go far:
Otherwise we spend our
Lives in a confusion
Of what we say and do with
    Who we really are.

You will any day now
Have this revelation:
"Why, we're all like people
    Acting in a play."
And will suffer, Johnny,
Man's unique temptation
Precisely at the moment
    You utter this cliché.

Remember if you can then,
Only the All-Father
Can change the cast or give them
    Easier lines to say;
Deliberate interference
With others for their own good
Is not allowed the author
    Of the play within The Play.

Just because our pride's an
Evil there's no end to,
Birthdays and the arts are
    Justified, for when
We consciously pretend to
Own the earth or play at
Being gods, thereby we
    Own that we are men.

As a human creature
You will all too often
Forget your proper station,
    Johnny, like us all;
Therefore let your birthday
Be a wild occasion
Like a Saturnalia
    Or a Servants' Ball.

What else shall I wish you?
Following convention
Shall I wish you Beauty
    Money, Happiness?
Or anything you mention?
No, for I recall an
Ancient proverb:—Nothing
    Fails like a success.

What limping devil sets our
Head and heart at variance,
That each time the Younger
        Generation sails,
The old and weather-beaten
Deny their own experience
And pray the gods to send them
        Calm seas, auspicious gales?

I'm not such an idiot
As to claim the power
To peer into the vistas
        Of your future, still
I'm prepared to guess you
Have not found your life as
Easy as your sister's
        And you never will.

If I'm right about this,
May you in your troubles,
Neither (like so many
        In the U.S.A.)
Be ashamed of any
Suffering as vulgar,
Nor bear them like a hero
        In the biggest way.

All the possibilities
It had to reject are
What give life and warmth to
        An actual character;
The roots of wit and charm tap
Secret springs of sorrow,
Every brilliant doctor
        Hides a murderer.

Then, since all self-knowledge
Tempts man into envy,
May you, by acquiring
　　　Proficiency in what
Whitehead calls the art of
Negative Prehension,
Love without desiring
　　　All that you are not.

Tao is a tightrope,
So to keep your balance,
May you always, Johnny,
　　　Manage to combine
Intellectual talents
With a sensual gusto,
The Socratic Doubt with
　　　The Socratic Sign.

That is all that I can
Think of at this moment
And it's time I brought these
　　　Verses to a close:
Happy Birthday, Johnny,
Live beyond your income,
Travel for enjoyment,
　　　Follow your own nose.

Shepherd's Carol

O lift your little pinkie
And touch the winter sky:
Love is all over the mountains
Where the beautiful go to die.

If Time were the wicked sheriff
    In a horse opera,
I'd pay for riding lessons
    And take his gun away.

If I were a Valentino
    And Fortune were a broad,
I'd hypnotise that iceberg
    Till she kissed me of her own accord.

If I'd stacked up the velvet
    And my crooked rib were dead,
I'd be breeding white canaries
    And eating crackers in bed.

But my cuffs are soiled and fraying
    The kitchen clock is slow,
And over the Blue Wonders
    The grass grew long ago.

I ain't speaking through the flowers
    Nor trying to explain,
But there ain't a living sorrow
    Comes wrapped in cellophane.

O solid is the sending
    Of the Boogie Woogie Man;
But who has found the horseshoes
    Or danced on Fiddler's Green?

O lift your little pinkie
  And touch the winter sky:
Love is all over the mountains
  Where the beautiful go to die.

Song of the Old Soldier

When the Sex War ended with the slaughter of the Grandmothers,
They found a bachelor's baby suffocating under them;
Somebody called him George and that was the end of it:
     They hitched him up to the Army.
     George, you old debutante,
     How did you get in the Army?

In the Retreat from Reason he deserted on his rocking-horse
And lived on a fairy's kindness till he tired of kicking her;
He smashed her spectacles and stole her check-book and mackintosh
     Then cruised his way back to the Army.
     George, you old numero,
     How did you get in the Army?

Before the Diet of Sugar he was using razor-blades
And exited soon after with an allergy to maidenheads;
He discovered a cure of his own, but no one would patent it,
     So he showed up again in the Army.
     George, you old flybynight,
     How did you get in the Army?

When the Vice Crusades were over he was hired by some Muscovites
Prospecting for deodorants among the Eskimos;
He was caught by a common cold and condemned to the whiskey
                                                     mines,
     But schemozzled back to the Army.
     George, you old Emperor,
     How did you get in the Army?

Since Peace was signed with Honour he's been minding his business;
But, whoops, here comes His Idleness, buttoning his uniform;
Just in tidy time to massacre the Innocents;
     He's come home to roost in the Army.
     George, you old matador,
     Welcome back to the Army.

Song of the Master and Boatswain

At Dirty Dick's and Sloppy Joe's
    We drank our liquor straight,
Some went upstairs with Margery,
    And some, alas, with Kate;
And two by two like cat and mouse
The homeless played at keeping house.

There Wealthy Meg, the Sailor's Friend,
    And Marion, cow-eyed,
Opened their arms to me but I
    Refused to step inside;
I was not looking for a cage
In which to mope in my old age.

The nightingales are sobbing in
    The orchards of our mothers,
And hearts that we broke long ago
    Have long been breaking others;
Tears are round, the sea is deep:
Roll them overboard and sleep.

Adrian and Francisco's Song

Adrian.

The lovely lawns are swarming
    With people no one knows,
And up the marble staircase run
A hundred maladjusted girls
    In sensible black hose,
For milk and fifteen minutes fun
Between Creative Leatherwork and
    Hygiene of The Nose.

Francisco.

Cupid no longer swishes,
    Venus no more behaves,
Committees take the earth in hand
To give the hills a thorough scrub
    And sterilize the waves;
The chef has died of horror, and
The war-horse and the battle-axe
    Have swept into their graves.

Chorus.

Well. Well. Well.
The Old World pooped at the party:
As the last waltz stopped, she whooped and flopped—
    "Small towns, my dear, are HELL."
Lay her out in her black silk pyjamas,
    Let down your hair and cry:
Good little sunbeams must learn to fly,
But it's madly ungay when the goldfish die.
    Well. Well. Well.

Miranda's Song

My Dear One is mine as mirrors are lonely,
As the poor and sad are real to the good king,
And the high green hill sits always by the sea.

Up jumped the Black Man behind the elder tree,
Turned a somersault and ran away waving;
My Dear One is mine as mirrors are lonely.

The Witch gave a squawk; her venomous body
Melted into light as water leaves a spring
And the high green hill sits always by the sea.

At his crossroads, too, the Ancient prayed for me;
Down his wasted cheeks tears of joy were running:
My Dear One is mine as mirrors are lonely.

He kissed me awake, and no one was sorry;
The sun shone on sails, eyes, pebbles, anything,
And the high green hill sits always by the sea.

So, to remember our changing garden, we
Are linked as children in a circle dancing:
My Dear One is mine as mirrors are lonely,
And the high green hill sits always by the sea.

Three Songs from *The Age of Anxiety*

Deep in my dark the dream shines
Yes, of you, you dear always;
My cause to cry, cold but my
Story still, still my music.

Mild rose the moon, moving through our
Naked nights: tonight it rains;
Black umbrellas blossom out;
Gone the gold, my golden ball.

Heavy these hands. I believed
That pleased pause, your pause was me
To love alone till life's end:
I thought this; this was not true.

You touched, you took. Tears fall. O
Fair my far, when far ago
Like waterwheels wishes spun
Radiant robes: but the robes tore.

. . .

When Laura lay on her ledger side
And nicely threw her north cheek up,
How pleasing the plight of her promising grove
And how rich the random I reached with a rise.

. . .

Hushed is the lake of hawks
Bright with our excitement,
And all the sky of skulls
Glows with scarlet roses;
The melter of men and salt
Admires the drinker of iron:
Bold banners of meaning
Blaze o'er the host of days.

Under Which Lyre

A REACTIONARY TRACT FOR THE TIMES

(Phi Beta Kappa Poem, Harvard, 1946)

Ares at last has quit the field,
The bloodstains on the bushes yield
    To seeping showers,
And in their convalescent state
The fractured towns associate
    With summer flowers.

Encamped upon the college plain
Raw veterans already train
    As freshman forces;
Instructors with sarcastic tongue
Shepherd the battle-weary young
    Through basic courses.

Among bewildering appliances
For mastering the arts and sciences
    They stroll or run,
And nerves that never flinched at slaughter
Are shot to pieces by the shorter
    Poems of Donne.

Professors back from secret missions
Resume their proper eruditions,
    Though some regret it;
They liked their dictaphones a lot,
They met some big wheels, and do not
    Let you forget it.

But Zeus' inscrutable decree
Permits the will-to-disagree
    To be pandemic,
Ordains that vaudeville shall preach
And every commencement speech
    Be a polemic.

Let Ares doze, that other war
Is instantly declared once more
    'Twixt those who follow
Precocious Hermes all the way
And those who without qualms obey
    Pompous Apollo.

Brutal like all Olympic games,
Though fought with smiles and Christian names
    And less dramatic,
This dialectic strife between
The civil gods is just as mean,
    And more fanatic.

What high immortals do in mirth
Is life and death on Middle Earth;
    Their a–historic
Antipathy forever gripes
All ages and somatic types,
    The sophomoric

Who face the future's darkest hints
With giggles or with prairie squints
    As stout as Cortez,
And those who like myself turn pale
As we approach with ragged sail
    The fattening forties.

The sons of Hermes love to play,
And only do their best when they
      Are told they oughtn't;
Apollo's children never shrink
From boring jobs but have to think
      Their work important.

Related by antithesis,
A compromise between us is
      Impossible;
Respect perhaps but friendship never:
Falstaff the fool confronts forever
      The prig Prince Hal.

If he would leave the self alone,
Apollo's welcome to the throne,
      Fasces and falcons;
He loves to rule, has always done it;
The earth would soon, did Hermes run it,
      Be like the Balkans.

But jealous of our god of dreams,
His common-sense in secret schemes
      To rule the heart;
Unable to invent the lyre,
Creates with simulated fire
      Official art.

And when he occupies a college,
Truth is replaced by Useful Knowledge;
      He pays particular
Attention to Commercial Thought,
Public Relations, Hygiene, Sport,
      In his curricula.

Athletic, extrovert and crude,
For him, to work in solitude
    Is the offence,
The goal a populous Nirvana:
His shield bears this device: *Mens sana*
    Qui mal y pense.

Today his arms, we must confess,
From Right to Left have met success,
    His banners wave
From Yale to Princeton, and the news
From Broadway to the Book Reviews
    Is very grave.

His radio Homers all day long
In over-Whitmanated song
    That does not scan,
With adjectives laid end to end,
Extol the doughnut and commend
    The Common Man.

His, too, each homely lyric thing
On sport or spousal love or spring
    Or dogs or dusters,
Invented by some court-house bard
For recitation by the yard
    In filibusters.

To him ascend the prize orations
And sets of fugal variations
    On some folk-ballad,
While dietitians sacrifice
A glass of prune-juice or a nice
    Marsh-mallow salad.

Charged with his compound of sensational
Sex plus some undenominational
            Religious matter,
Enormous novels by co-eds
Rain down on our defenceless heads
            Till our teeth chatter.

In fake Hermetic uniforms
Behind our battle-line, in swarms
            That keep alighting,
His existentialists declare
That they are in complete despair,
            Yet go on writing.

No matter; He shall be defied;
White Aphrodite is on our side:
            What though his threat
To organize us grow more critical?
Zeus willing, we, the unpolitical,
            Shall beat him yet.

Lone scholars, sniping from the walls
Of learned periodicals,
            Our facts defend,
Our intellectual marines,
Landing in little magazines
            Capture a trend.

By night our student Underground
At cocktail parties whisper round
            From ear to ear;
Fat figures in the public eye
Collapse next morning, ambushed by
            Some witty sneer.

In our morale must lie our strength:
So, that we may behold at length
      Routed Apollo's
Battalions melt away like fog,
Keep well the Hermetic Decalogue,
      Which runs as follows:—

Thou shalt not do as the dean pleases,
Thou shalt not write thy doctor's thesis
      On education,
Thou shalt not worship projects nor
Shalt thou or thine bow down before
      Administration.

Thou shalt not answer questionnaires
Or quizzes upon World-Affairs,
      Nor with compliance
Take any test. Thou shalt not sit
With statisticians nor commit
      A social science.

Thou shalt not be on friendly terms
With guys in advertising firms,
      Nor speak with such
As read the Bible for its prose,
Nor, above all, make love to those
      Who wash too much.

Thou shalt not live within thy means
Nor on plain water and raw greens.
      If thou must choose
Between the chances, choose the odd;
Read *The New Yorker,* trust in God;
      And take short views.

Nursery Rhyme

Their learned kings bent down to chat with frogs;
This was until the Battle of the Bogs.
The key that opens is the key that rusts.

Their cheerful kings made toffee on their stoves;
This was until the Rotting of the Loaves.
The robins vanish when the ravens come.

That was before the coaches reached the bogs;
Now woolly bears pursue the spotted dogs.
A witch can make an ogre out of mud.

That was before the weevils ate the loaves;
Now blinded bears invade the orange groves.
A witch can make an ogre out of mud.

The woolly bears have polished off the dogs;
Our bowls of milk are full of drowning frogs.
The robins vanish when the ravens come.

The blinded bears have rooted up the groves;
Our poisoned milk boils over on our stoves.
The key that opens is the key that rusts.

Barcarolle

(*Aria from* The Rake's Progress)

Gently, little boat,
Across the waters float,
Their crystal waves dividing;
    The sun in the west
    Is going to rest:
        Glide, glide, glide,
Towards the Islands of the Blest.

Orchards greenly grace
That undisturbèd place,
The wearied soul recalling
    To slumber and dream,
    While many a stream
        Falls, falls, falls,
Descanting on a child-like theme.

Lion, lamb and deer,
Untouched by greed or fear,
About its woods are straying,
    And quietly now
    The blossoming bough
        Sways, sways, sways
Above the clear unclouded brow.

Music Ho

The Emperor's favorite concubine
    Was in the Eunuch's pay,
The Wardens of the Marches turned
    Their spears the other way;
The vases crack, the ladies die,
    The Oracles are wrong:
We suck our thumbs or sleep; the show
    Is gamey and too long.

But—Music Ho!—at last it comes,
    The Transformation Scene:
A rather scruffy-looking god
    Descends in a machine
And, gabbling off his rustic rhymes,
    Misplacing one or two,
Commands the prisoners to walk,
    The enemies to screw.

The Love Feast

In an upper room at midnight
See us gathered on behalf
Of love according to the gospel
Of the radio-phonograph.

Lou is telling Anne what Molly
Said to Mark behind her back;
Jack likes Jill who worships George
Who has the hots for Jack.

Catechumens make their entrance;
Steep enthusiastic eyes
Flicker after tits and baskets;
Someone vomits; someone cries.

Willy cannot bear his father,
Lilian is afraid of kids;
The Love that rules the sun and stars
Permits what He forbids.

Adrian's pleasure-loving dachshund
In a sinner's lap lies curled;
Drunken absent-minded fingers
Pat a sinless world.

Who is Jenny lying to
By long-distance telephone?
The Love that made her out of nothing
Tells me to go home.

But that Miss Number in the corner
Playing hard to get. . . .
I am sorry I'm not sorry . . .
Make me chaste, Lord, but not yet.

Song

Deftly, admiral, cast your fly
    Into the slow deep hover,
Till the wise old trout mistake and die;
    Salt are the deeps that cover
    The glittering fleets you led,
        White is your head.

Read on, ambassador, engrossed
    In your favourite Stendhal;
The Outer Provinces are lost,
    Unshaven horsemen swill
    The great wines of the Châteaux
        Where you danced long ago.

Do not turn, do not lift, your eyes
    Toward the still pair standing
On the bridge between your properties,
    Indifferent to your minding:
    In its glory, in its power,
        This is their hour.

Nothing your strength, your skill, could do
    Can alter their embrace
Or dispersuade the Furies who
    At the appointed place
    With claw and dreadful brow
        Wait for them now.

Limericks

A friend, who is not an ascetic,
Writes: "Ireland, my dear, is *magnetic*.
   No snakes. Lots of elves
   Who just OFFER themselves—
Rather small but MOST sympathetic."

. . .

A Young Person came out of the mists
Who had the most beautiful wrists:
   A scandal occurred
   Which has long been interred,
But the legend about them persists.

. . .

After vainly invoking the Muse,
A poet cried: "Hell, what's the use?
   There's more inspiration
   At Grand Central Station;
I shall go there this moment and cruise."

. . .

Said the Queen to the King: "I don't frown on
The fact that you choose to go down on
   My page on the stairs
   But you'll give the boy airs
If you *will* do the job with your crown on."

. . .

T. S. Eliot is quite at a loss
When clubwomen bustle across
    At literary teas,
    Crying: "What, if you please,
Did you mean by *The Mill on the Floss*?"

. . .

The Bishop-Elect of Hong Kong
Has a cock which is ten inches long;
    He thinks the spectators
    Are admiring his gaiters
When he goes to the Gents—he is wrong.

. . .

There was a young poet whose sex
Was aroused by aesthetic effects;
    Marvell's *The Garden*
    Gave him a hard-on
And he came during *Oedipus Rex*.

. . .

To get the Last Poems of Yeats,
You need not mug up on dates;
    All a reader requires
    Is some knowledge of gyres
And the sort of people he hates.

Hunting Season

A shot: from crag to crag
    The tell-tale echoes trundle;
Some feathered he-or-she
    Is now a lifeless bundle
And, proud into a kitchen, some
Example of our tribe will come.

Down in the startled valley
    Two lovers break apart:
He hears the roaring oven
    Of a witch's heart;
Behind his murmurs of her name
She sees a marksman taking aim.

Reminded of the hour
    And that his chair is hard,
A deathless verse half done,
    One interrupted bard
Postpones his dying with a dish
Of several suffocated fish.

The Willow-Wren and the Stare

A starling and a willow-wren,
    On a may-tree by a weir,
Saw them meet and heard him say;
    "Dearest of my dear,
More lively than these waters chortling
    As they leap the dam,
My sweetest duck, my precious goose,
    My white lascivious lamb."
With a smile she listened to him;
    Talking to her there:
What does he want? said the willow-wren;
    Much too much, said the stare.

"Forgive these loves who dwell in me,
    These brats of greed and fear,
The honking bottom-pinching clown,
    The snivelling sonneteer,
That so, between us, even these,
    Who till the grave are mine,
For all they fall so short of may,
    Dear heart, be still a sign."
With a smile she closed her eyes,
    Silent she lay there:
Does he mean what he says? said the willow-wren;
    Some of it, said the stare.

"Hark! Wild Robin winds his horn
    And, as his notes require,
Now our laughter-loving spirits
    Must in awe retire
And let their kinder partners,
    Speechless with desire,
Go in their holy selfishness,
    Unfunny to the fire."

Smiling, silently she threw
      Her arms about him there:
Is it only that? said the willow-wren;
      It's that as well, said the stare.

Waking in her arms he cried,
      Utterly content;
"I have heard the high good noises,
      Promoted for an instant,
Stood upon the shining outskirts
      Of that Joy I thank
For you, my dog and every goody."
      There on the grass bank
She laughed, he laughed, they laughed together,
      Then they ate and drank:
Did he know what he meant? said the willow-wren
      God only knows, said the stare.

The Proof

"When rites and melodies begin
  To alter modes and times,
And timid bar-flies boast aloud
  Of uncommitted crimes,
And leading families are proud
  To dine with their black sheep,
What promises, what discipline,
  If any, will Love keep?"
    So roared Fire on their right:
      But Tamino and Pamina
      Walked past its rage,
    Sighing O, sighing O,
  In timeless fermatas of awe and delight
    (Innocent? Yes. Ignorant? No.)
    Down the grim passage.

"When stinking Chaos lifts the latch,
  And Grotte backward spins,
And Helen's nose becomes a beak,
  And cats and dogs grow chins,
And daisies claw and pebbles shriek,
  And Form and Color part,
What swarming hatreds then will hatch
  Out of Love's riven heart."
    So hissed Water on their left:
      But Pamina and Tamino
      Opposed its spite,
    With his worship, with her sweetness—
  O look now! See how they emerge from the cleft
    (Frightened? No. Happy? Yes.)
    Out into sunlight.

"The Truest Poetry Is the Most Feigning"

(For Edgar Wind)

By all means sing of love but, if you do,
Please make a rare old proper hullabaloo:
When ladies ask *How much do you love me?*
The Christian answer is *così-così*.
But poets are not celibate divines;
Had Dante said so, who would read his lines?
Be subtle, various, ornamental, clever,
And do not listen to those critics ever
Whose crude provincial gullets crave in books
Plain cooking made still plainer by plain cooks,
As though the Muse preferred her half-wit sons;
Good poets have a weakness for bad puns.

Suppose your Beatrice be, as usual, late,
And you would tell us how it feels to wait,
You're free to think, what may be even true,
You're so in love that one hour seems like two,
But write—*As I sat waiting for her call,*
Each second longer darker seemed than all
(Something like this but more elaborate still)
Those raining centuries it took to fill
That quarry whence Endymion's love was torn;
From such ingenious fibs are poems born:
Then, should she leave you for some other guy,
Or ruin you with debts, or go and die,
No metaphor, remember, can express
A real historical unhappiness;
Your tears have value if they make us gay;
O Happy Grief! is all sad verse can say.

The living girl's your business (some odd sorts
Have been an inspiration to men's thoughts):
Yours may be old enough to be your mother,
Or have one leg that's shorter than the other,

Or play Lacrosse or do the Modern Dance;
To you that's destiny, to us it's chance;
We cannot love your love till she take on,
Through you, the wonders of a paragon.
Sing her triumphant passage to our land,
The sun her footstool, the moon in her right hand,
And seven planets blazing in her hair,
Queen of the Night and Empress of the Air;
Tell how her fleet by nine king swans is led,
Wild geese write magic letters overhead
And hippocampi follow in her wake
With Amphisbaene, gentle for her sake;
Sing her descent on the exulting shore
To bless the vines and put an end to war.

If half-way through such praises of your dear,
Riot and shooting fill the streets with fear,
And overnight, as in some terror dream,
Poets are suspect with the New Regime,
Stick at your desk and hold your panic in;
What you are writing may still save your skin:
Re-sex the pronouns, add a few details,
And, lo, a panegyric ode which hails
(How is the Censor, bless his heart, to know?)
The new pot-bellied Generalissimo.
Some epithets, of course, like *lily-breasted*
Need modifying to, say, *lion-chested,*
A title *Goddess of wry-necks and wrens*
To *Great Reticulator of the fens,*
But in an hour your poem qualifies
For a State pension or His annual prize,
And you will die in bed (which He will not:
That silly sausage will be hanged or shot).
Though honest Iagos, true to form, will write
Shame! in your margins, *Toady! Hypocrite!,*
True hearts, clear heads will hear the note of glory
And put inverted commas round the story,
Thinking—*Old Sly-boots! We shall never know
Her name or nature. Well, it's better so.*

For, given Man, by birth, by education,
Imago Dei who forgot his station,
The self-made creature who himself unmakes,
The only creature ever made who fakes,
With no more nature in his loving smile
Than in his theories of a natural style,
What but tall tales, the luck of verbal playing,
Can trick his lying nature into saying
That love, or truth in any serious sense,
Like orthodoxy, is a reticence.

Nocturne

Make this night loveable,
Moon, and with eye single
Looking down from up there,
Bless me, One especial
And friends everywhere.

With a cloudless brightness
Surround our absences;
Innocent be our sleeps,
Watched by great still spaces,
White hills, glittering deeps.

Parted by circumstance,
Grant each your indulgence
That we may meet in dreams
For talk, for dalliance,
By warm hearths, by cool streams.

Shine lest tonight any,
In the dark suddenly,
Wake alone in a bed
To hear his own fury
Wishing his love were dead.

Metalogue to *The Magic Flute*

(Lines composed in commemoration of the Mozart Bicentenary.
To be spoken by the singer playing the role of Sarastro.)

Relax, Maestro, put your baton down:
Only the fogiest of the old will frown
If you the trials of the *Prince* prorogue
To let *Sarastro* speak this Metalogue,
A form acceptable to us, although
Unclassed by *Aristotle* or *Boileau.*
No modern audience finds it incorrect,
For interruption is what we expect
Since that new god, the Paid Announcer, rose,
Who with his quasi-Ossianic prose
Cuts in upon the lovers, halts the band,
To name a sponsor or to praise a brand.
Not that I have a product to describe
That you could wear or cook with or imbibe;
You cannot hoard or waste a work of art:
I come to praise but not to sell *Mozart,*
Who came into this world of war and woe
At Salzburg just two centuries ago,
When kings were many and machines were few,
And open Atheism something new.
(It makes a servantless New Yorker sore
To think sheer Genius had to stand before
A mere Archbishop with uncovered head:
But *Mozart* never had to make his bed.)

The history of Music as of Man
Will not go cancrizans, and no ear can
Recall what, when the Archduke *Francis* reigned,
Was heard by ears whose treasure-hoard contained
A *Flute* already but as yet no *Ring*:
Each age has its own mode of listening.
We know the *Mozart* of our fathers' time
Was gay, rococo, sweet, but not sublime,

A Viennese Italian; that is changed
Since music critics learned to feel "estranged";
Now it's the Germans he is classed amongst,
A *Geist* whose music was composed from *Angst,*
At International Festivals enjoys
An equal status with the Twelve-Tone Boys;
He awes the lovely and the very rich,
And even those *Divertimenti* which
He wrote to play while bottles were uncorked,
Milord chewed noisily, Milady talked,
Are heard in solemn silence, score on knees,
Like quartets by the deafest of the *B*'s.
What next? One can no more imagine how,
In concert halls two hundred years from now,
When the Mozartian sound-waves move the air,
The cognoscenti will be moved, than dare
Predict how high orchestral pitch will go,
How many tones will constitute a row,
The tempo at which regimented feet
Will march about the Moon, the form of Suite
For Piano in a Post-Atomic Age,
Prepared by some contemporary *Cage.*

An opera composer may be vexed
By later umbrage taken at his text:
Even *Macaulay*'s schoolboy knows today
What *Robert Graves* or *Margaret Mead* would say
About the status of the sexes in this play,
Writ in that era of barbaric dark
'Twixt Modern Mom and Bronze-Age Matriarch.
Where now the Roman Fathers and their creed?
"Ah, where," sighs *Mr Mitty,* "Where indeed?"
And glances sideways at his vital spouse
Whose rigid jaw-line and contracted brows
Express her scorn and utter detestation
For Roman views of Female Education.
In Nineteen Fifty-Six we find the *Queen*
A highly-paid and most efficient Dean
(Who, as we all know, really runs the College),

Sarastro, tolerated for his knowledge,
Teaching the History of Ancient Myth
At *Bryn Mawr, Vassar, Bennington* or *Smith;*
Pamina may a *Time* researcher be
To let *Tamino* take his Ph.D.,
Acquiring manly wisdom as he wishes
While changing diapers and doing dishes;
Sweet *Papagena,* when she's time to spare,
Listens to *Mozart* operas on the air,
Though *Papageno,* one is sad to feel,
Prefers the juke box to the glockenspiel,
And how is—what was easy in the past—
A democratic villain to be cast?
Monostatos must make his bad impression
Without a race, religion or profession.

A work that lasts two hundred years is tough,
And operas, God knows, must stand enough:
What greatness made, small vanities abuse.
What must they not endure? The Diva whose
Fioriture and climactic note
The silly old composer never wrote,
Conductor *X,* that overrated bore
Who alters tempi and who cuts the score,
Director *Y* who with ingenious wit
Places his wretched singers in the pit
While dancers mime their roles, *Z* the Designer
Who sets the whole thing on an ocean liner,
The girls in shorts, the men in yachting caps;
Yet Genius triumphs over all mishaps,
Survives a greater obstacle than these,
Translation into foreign Operese
(English sopranos are condemned to *languish*
Because our tenors have to hide their *anguish*);
It soothes the *Frank,* it stimulates the *Greek:*
Genius surpasses all things, even Chic.
We who know nothing—which is just as well—
About the future, can, at least, foretell,
Whether they live in air-borne nylon cubes,

Practice group-marriage or are fed through tubes,
That crowds two centuries from now will press
(Absurd their hair, ridiculous their dress)
And pay in currencies, however weird,
To hear *Sarastro* booming through his beard,
Sharp connoisseurs approve if it is clean
The F in alt of the *Nocturnal Queen,*
Some uncouth creature from the *Bronx* amaze
Park Avenue by knowing all the *K*'s.

How seemly, then, to celebrate the birth
Of one who did no harm to our poor earth,
Created masterpieces by the dozen,
Indulged in toilet humor with his cousin
And had a pauper's funeral in the rain,
The like of whom we shall not see again:
How comely, also, to forgive; we should,
As *Mozart,* were he living, surely would,
Remember kindly *Salieri*'s shade,
Accused of murder and his works unplayed,
Nor, while we praise the dead, should we forget
We have *Stravinsky*—bless him!—with us yet.
{ Basta! Maestro, make your minions play!
In all hearts, as in our finale, may
Reason & Love be crowned, assume their rightful sway.

A Toast

(Christ Church Gaudy, 1960)

What on earth does one say at a Gaudy,
    On such an occasion as this,
O what, since I may not be bawdy,
    Can I do except reminisce?
Middle-age with its glasses and dentures
    (There's an opera about it by Strauss)
Puts an end to romantic adventures,
    But not to my love of *The House*.

Ah! those Twenties before I was twenty,
    When the news never gave one the glooms,
When the chef had minions in plenty,
    And we could have lunch in our rooms.
In *Peck* there were marvelous parties
    With bubbly and brandy and grouse,
And the aesthetes fought with the hearties:
    It was fun, then, to be at *The House*.

National Service had not been suggested,
    O-Level and A were called Certs,
Our waistcoats were cut double-breasted,
    Our flannel trousers like skirts.
One could meet any day in Society
    Harold Acton, Tom Driberg or *Rowse*:
May there always, to lend their variety,
    Be some rather odd fish at *The House*.

The *Clarendon*'s gone—I regret her—
    The *George* is closed and forgot;
Some changes are all for the better,
    But *Woolworth*'s is probably not.
May the *Meadows* be only frequented
    By scholars and couples and cows:
God save us from all these demented
    Plans for a road through *The House*.

All those who wish well to our College
    Will wish her *Treasurer* well;
May Mammon give him foreknowledge
    Of just what to buy and to sell,
That all his investments on which her
    Income depends may be wows:
May She ever grow richer and richer,
    And the gravy abound at *The House*.

God bless and keep out of quarrels
    The *Dean*, the *Chapter* and *D*,
The *Censors* who shepherd our morals,
    Roy, *Hooky*, *Little* and me.
May those who come up next October
    Be *anständig*, have *esprit* and *nous*:
And now, though not overly sober,
    I give you a toast—TO THE HOUSE!

Some Thirty Inches from My Nose

Some thirty inches from my nose
The frontier of my Person goes,
And all the untilled air between
Is private *pagus* or demesne.
Stranger, unless with bedroom eyes
I beckon you to fraternize,
Beware of rudely crossing it:
I have no gun, but I can spit.

On the Circuit

Among pelagian travelers,
Lost on their lewd conceited way
To Massachusetts, Michigan,
Miami or L.A.,

An airborne instrument I sit,
Predestined nightly to fulfill
Columbia-Giesen-Management's
Unfathomable will,

By whose election justified,
I bring my gospel of the Muse
To fundamentalists, to nuns,
To Gentiles and to Jews,

And daily, seven days a week,
Before a local sense has jelled,
From talking-site to talking-site
Am jet-or-prop-propelled.

Though warm my welcome everywhere,
I shift so frequently, so fast,
I cannot now say where I was
The evening before last,

Unless some singular event
Should intervene to save the place,
A truly asinine remark,
A soul-bewitching face,

Or blessed encounter, full of joy,
Unscheduled on the Giesen Plan,
With, here, an addict of Tolkien,
There, a Charles Williams fan.

Since Merit but a dunghill is,
I mount the rostrum unafraid:
Indeed, 'twere damnable to ask
If I am overpaid.

Spirit is willing to repeat
Without a qualm the same old talk,
But Flesh is homesick for our snug
Apartment in New York.

A sulky fifty-six, he finds
A change of mealtime utter hell,
Grown far too crotchety to like
A luxury hotel.

The Bible is a goodly book
I always can peruse with zest,
But really cannot say the same
For Hilton's *Be My Guest,*

Nor bear with equanimity
The radio in students' cars,
Musak at breakfast, or—dear God!—
Girl-organists in bars.

Then, worst of all, the anxious thought,
Each time my plane begins to sink
And the No Smoking sign comes on:
What will there be to drink?

Is this a milieu where I must
How grahamgreeneish! How infra dig!
Snatch from the bottle in my bag
An analeptic swig?

Another morning comes: I see,
Dwindling below me on the plain,
The roofs of one more audience
I shall not see again.

God bless the lot of them, although
I don't remember which was which:
God bless the U.S.A., so large,
So friendly, and so rich.

Song of the Ogres

Little fellow, you're amusing,
Stop before you end by losing
    Your shirt:
Run along to Mother, Gus,
Those who interfere with us
    Get hurt.

Honest Virtue, old wives prattle,
Always wins the final battle.
    Dear, Dear!
Life's exactly what it looks,
Love may triumph in the books,
    Not here.

We're not joking, we assure you:
Those who rode this way before you
    Died hard.
What? Still spoiling for a fight?
Well, you've asked for it all right:
    On guard!

Always hopeful, aren't you? Don't be.
Night is falling and it won't be
    Long now:
You will never see the dawn,
You will wish you'd not been born.
    And how!

Song of the Devil

Ever since observation taught me temptation
Is a matter of timing, I've tried
To clothe my fiction in up-to-date diction,
The contemporary jargon of Pride.
    I can recall when, to win the more
        Obstinate round,
    The best bet was to say to them: "Sin the more
        That Grace may abound."

Since Social Psychology replaced Theology
The process goes twice as quick,
If a conscience is tender and loth to surrender
I have only to whisper: "You're sick!"
    Puritanical morality
        Is madly Non-U:
    Enhance your personality
        With a Romance, with two.

"If you pass up a dame, you've yourself to blame,
For shame is neurotic, so snatch!
All rules are too formal, in fact they're abnormal,
For any desire is natch.
    So take your proper share, man, of
        Dope and drink:
    Aren't you the Chairman of
        Ego, Inc?

"Free-Will is a mystical myth as statistical
Methods have objectively shown,
A fad of the Churches: since the latest researches
Into Motivation it's known
    That Honour is hypocrisy,
        Honesty a joke.
    You live in a Democracy:
        Lie like other folk.

"Since men are like goods, what are shouldn'ts or shoulds
When you are the Leading Brand?
Let them all drop dead, you're way ahead,
Beat them up if they dare to demand
What may your intention be,
Or what might ensue:
There's a difference of dimension be-
tween the rest and you.

"If in the scrimmage of business your image
Should ever tarnish or stale,
Public Relations can take it and make it
Shine like a Knight of the Grail.
You can mark up the price that you sell at, if
Your package has glamour and show:
Values are relative.
Dough is dough.

"So let each while you may think you're more O.K.,
More yourself than anyone else,
Till you find that you're hooked, your goose is cooked,
And you're only a cypher of Hell's.
Believe while you can that I'm proud of you,
Enjoy your dream:
I'm so bored with the whole fucking crowd of you
I could *scream*!"

The Geography of the House

(For Christopher Isherwood)

Seated after breakfast
In this white-tiled cabin
Arabs call *The House where
Everybody goes,*
Even melancholics
Raise a cheer to Mrs
Nature for the primal
Pleasures She bestows.

Sex is but a dream to
Seventy-and-over,
But a joy proposed un–
-til we start to shave:
Mouth-delight depends on
Virtue in the cook, but
This She guarantees from
Cradle unto grave.

Lifted off the potty,
Infants from their mothers
Hear their first impartial
Words of worldly praise:
Hence, to start the morning
With a satisfactory
Dump is a good omen
All our adult days.

Revelation came to
Luther in a privy
(Cross-words have been solved there):
Rodin was no fool
When he cast his Thinker,
Cogitating deeply,
Crouched in the position
Of a man at stool.

All the Arts derive from
This ur-act of making,
Private to the artist:
Makers' lives are spent
Striving in their chosen
Medium to produce a
De-narcissus-ised en-
-during excrement.

Freud did not invent the
Constipated miser:
Banks have letter-boxes
Built in their façade
Marked *For Night Deposits,*
Stocks are firm or liquid,
Currencies of nations
Either soft or hard.

Global Mother, keep our
Bowels of compassion
Open through our lifetime,
Purge our minds as well:
Grant us a kind ending,
Not a second childhood,
Petulant, weak-sphinctered,
In a cheap hotel.

Keep us in our station:
When we get pound-noteish,
When we seem about to
Take up Higher Thought,
Send us some deflating
Image like the pained ex-
-pression on a Major
Prophet taken short.

(Orthodoxy ought to
Bless our modern plumbing:
Swift and St Augustine
Lived in centuries
When a stench of sewage
Ever in the nostrils
Made a strong debating
Point for Manichees.)

Mind and Body run on
Different time-tables:
Not until our morning
Visit here can we
Leave the dead concerns of
Yesterday behind us,
Face with all our courage
What is now to be.

Moralities

(Text After Aesop: Music by Hans Werner Henze)

I

Speaker.
In the First Age the frogs dwelt
At peace in their pond: they paddled about,
Flies they caught and fat grew.

Courts they knew not, nor kings nor servants,
No laws they had, nor police nor jails:
All were equal, happy together.

The days went by in an unbroken calm:
Bored they grew, ungrateful for
Their good-luck, began to murmur.

Chorus.
   Higgledy-Piggledy,
   What our Society
   Needs is more Discipline,
   Form and Degree.
   Nobody wants to live
   Anachronistically:
   Lions have a Hierarchy,
   Why shouldn't we?

Speaker.
To mighty Jove on his jewelled throne
Went the Frog-Folk, the foolish people:
Thus they cried in chorus together.

Chorus.
Hickory-Dockery,
Greatest Olympian,
Graciously grant the petition we bring.

Life as we know it is
Unsatisfactory,
We want a Monarchy,
Give us a King!

Bass Solo.
Foolish children, your choice is unwise.
But so be it: go back and wait.

Speaker.
Into their pond from the heavens above,
With a splendid splash that sprayed them all,
Something fell, then floated around.

From the edge of their pond in awe they gazed,
The Frog-Folk, the foolish people:
Words they awaited, but no words came.

Chorus.
He has no legs. He has no head.
Is he dumb? Is he deaf? Is he blind? Is he dead?
It's not a man. It's not a frog.
Why, it's nothing but a rotten old log!
Silly stump, watch me jump!
Tee-hee-hee, you can't catch me!
Boo to you! Boo! Boo! Boo!

Speaker.
Back to Jove on his jewelled throne
Went the Frog-Folk, the foolish people:
Thus they cried in chorus together.

Chorus.
Jiggery-Pokery,
Jove, you've insulted the
Feelings of every
Sensitive frog:

What we demand is a
Plenipotentiary
Sovereign, not an in-
animate log.

Bass Solo.

By the hard way must the unwise learn.
So be it: go back and wait.

Speaker.

On their pond from the heavens above,
Cruel-beaked, a crane alighted.
Fierce, ravenous, a frog-eater.

Doom was upon them, Dread seized
The Frog-Folk, the foolish people:
They tried to escape. It was too late.

Chorus.

No! No! Woe! Woe! O! O! O. . . .

Speaker.

If people are too dumb to know when all is well with them,
The gods shrug their shoulders and say:—To Hell with them.

II

Speaker.

When first had no second, before Time was,
Mistress Kind, the Mother of all things,
Summoned the crows: they crowded before Her.

Alto Solo.

Dun must you be, not dainty to behold,
For your gain, though, I grace you with the gift of song:
Well shall you warble, as welcome to the ear
As the lively lark or loud nightingale.
Go in peace.

Speaker.

Gaily they went,
And daily at dawn with dulcet voices
Tooted in the tree-tops a tuneful madrigal.

Chorus.

Now, glorious in the East, the day is breaking:
Creatures of field and forest, from your sleep awaking,
Consort your voices, fearless of exposure,
And of yourselves now make a free disclosure,
Your pitch of presence to the world proclaiming,
Expressing, affirming, uttering and naming,
And each in each full recognition finding
No scornful echo but a warm responding,
Your several notes not harsh nor interfering,
But all in joy and concord co-inhering.

Speaker.

So they chanted till by chance one day
Came within earshot where the crows were nesting
A stand of horses, stallions and mares,
Whinneying and neighing as their wont in Spring is.

Chorus.

How strange! How astonishing! What astonishing sounds!
Never have we heard such noises as these.
It's so . . . so . . . so . . . so . . . so IT!
How new, How new! We must be too. What a break-through!
Away with dominant and tonic!
Let's be chic and electronic.
Down with the Establishment!
Up with non-music, the Sound-Event!
Arias are out and neighing is in:
Hurrah for horses! Let us begin.

Speaker.

But crows are no more horses than chutney is tabasco:
Their efforts at *aggiornomento* ended in fiasco.

Chorus.
CAW! CAW! CAW! CAW! CAW!

III

Speaker.
A ship put to sea, sailed out of harbour
On a peaceful morning with passengers aboard.
The sun was shining, but the ship's Captain,
Weather-wise, watching the sky,
Warned his crew.

Bass Solo.
Wild will be tonight
With a gurling gale and great waves.
To your storm stations! Stand by!

Chorus.
O Captain, Captain, tell us the truth!
Are we doomed to drown in the deep sea?

Bass Solo.
While my body breathes I will battle for our lives,
But our fate lies now in Neptune's hands.

Chorus.
Ah! What shall we do? The ship is about to founder,
Overwhelmed by the waves that so wildly surround her.
Neptune at our sins is righteously offended:
Over the deck his dreadful trident is extended.

Neptune, Neptune, forgive us! We confess it sadly,
We have neglected Thy worship and acted very badly.
Forgive us! Have mercy, have mercy, and be our Saviour,
And for ever after we will alter our behaviour.

Neptune, thou Strong One, stop this outrageous welter,
Restrain the wind and waft us safely into shelter:
Bulls we will bring to Thine altar and incense offer,
With treasures of great price fill up Thy temple coffer.

Bass Solo.

The wind is falling, the waves are less,
The clouds scatter, the sky lightens:
By the kindness of Neptune we have come through.

Chorus.

We knew He was joking, not serious:
Who would harm nice people like us?

In this merry month of May,
　　Dew on leaves a-sparkle,
Of youth and love and laughter sing,
　　Dancing in a circle.

Over hill, over dale,
　　Over the wide water,
Jack McGrew is come to woo
　　Jill, the oil-king's daughter.

Come from afar in his motor-car,
　　Eager to show devotion,
Looking so cute in his Sunday Suit,
　　And smelling of shaving-lotion.

Here comes the Bride at her Father's side,
　　Fresh as thyme or parsley:
Blushing now, to the Bridegroom's bow
　　She answers with a curtsey.

Boys Semi-Chorus.

Kiss her once, kiss her twice,
　　Bring her orchids on a salver,
Spit in her eye if she starts to cry,
　　And send her to Charlie Colver.

Girls Semi-Chorus.

Feed the brute with eggs and fruit,
            Keep him clean and tidy,
Give him what-for if he starts to snore,
            And scold him every Friday.

Chorus.

We wish you health, we wish you wealth,
            And seven smiling children,
Silver-bright be every night,
            And every day be golden.

Captain, why do you sit apart,
Frowning over your nautical chart?
Blue is the sky and bright is the sun:
Leave your bridge and join the fun.

Bass Solo.

The sky is blue, the sun is bright,
But who laughs in the morning may weep before night.

Chorus.

Your gloom does not enlighten us:
We will not let you frighten us.

An acid-drop for the Corner Cop,
            A crab-apple for Teacher,
Some mouldy fudge for His Honour the Judge,
            And a Bronx Cheer for the Preacher.

Speaker.

When afraid, men pray to the gods in all sincerity,
But worship only themselves in their days of prosperity.

A New Year Greeting

(After an Article by Mary J. Marples in
Scientific American, *January 1969)*

(For Vassily Yanowsky)

On this day tradition allots
    to taking stock of our lives,
my greetings to all of you, Yeasts,
    Bacteria, Viruses,
Aerobics and Anaerobics:
    A Very Happy New Year
to all for whom my ectoderm
    is as Middle-Earth to me.

For creatures your size I offer
    a free choice of habitat,
so settle yourselves in the zone
    that suits you best, in the pools
of my pores or the tropical
    forests of arm-pit and crotch,
in the deserts of my fore-arms,
    or the cool woods of my scalp.

Build colonies: I will supply
    adequate warmth and moisture,
the sebum and lipids you need,
    on condition you never
do me annoy with your presence,
    but behave as good guests should,
not rioting into acne
    or athlete's-foot or a boil.

Does my inner weather affect
        the surfaces where you live?
Do unpredictable changes
        record my rocketing plunge
from fairs when the mind is in tift
        and relevant thoughts occur
to fouls when nothing will happen
        and no one calls and it rains.

I should like to think that I make
        a not impossible world,
but an Eden it cannot be:
        my games, my purposive acts,
may turn to catastrophes there.
        If you were religious folk,
how would your dramas justify
        unmerited suffering?

By what myths would your priests account
        for the hurricanes that come
twice every twenty-four hours,
        each time I dress or undress,
when, clinging to keratin rafts,
        whole cities are swept away
to perish in space, or the Flood
        that scalds to death when I bathe?

Then, sooner or later, will dawn
        a day of Apocalypse,
when my mantle suddenly turns
        too cold, too rancid, for you,
appetising to predators
        of a fiercer sort, and I
am stripped of excuse and nimbus,
        a Past, subject to Judgement.

Doggerel by a Senior Citizen

(For Robert Lederer)

Our earth in 1969
Is not the planet I call mine,
The world, I mean, that gives me strength
To hold off chaos at arm's length.

My Eden landscapes and their climes
Are constructs from Edwardian times,
When bath-rooms took up lots of space,
And, before eating, one said Grace.

The automobile, the aeroplane,
Are useful gadgets, but profane:
The enginry of which I dream
Is moved by water or by steam.

Reason requires that I approve
The light-bulb which I cannot love:
To me more reverence-commanding
A fish-tail burner on the landing.

My family ghosts I fought and routed,
Their values, though, I never doubted:
I thought their Protestant Work-Ethic
Both practical and sympathetic.

When couples played or sang duets,
It was immoral to have debts:
I shall continue till I die
To pay in cash for what I buy.

The Book of Common Prayer we knew
Was that of 1662:
Though with-it sermons may be well,
Liturgical reforms are hell.

Sex was, of course—it always is—
The most enticing of mysteries,
But news-stands did not yet supply
Manichaean pornography.

Then Speech was mannerly, an Art,
Like learning not to belch or fart:
I cannot settle which is worse,
The Anti-Novel or Free Verse.

Nor are those Ph.D.'s my kith,
Who dig the symbol and the myth:
I count myself a man of letters
Who writes, or hopes to, for his betters.

Dare any call Permissiveness
An educational success?
Saner those class-rooms which I sat in,
Compelled to study Greek and Latin.

Though I suspect the term is crap,
If there *is* a Generation Gap,
Who is to blame? Those, old or young,
Who will not learn their Mother-Tongue.

But Love, at least, is not a state
Either *en vogue* or out-of-date,
And I've true friends, I will allow,
To talk and eat with here and now.

Me alienated? Bosh! It's just
As a sworn citizen who must
Skirmish with it that I feel
Most at home with what is Real.

Notes

AND

Index of Titles and First Lines

Notes

Except for previously unpublished or uncollected poems, the texts in this book are based on the early printed editions, with corrections from manuscripts and other sources. The texts do not reflect the cuts and changes Auden made for his later collected editions. Where a poem had no title in the early editions, the title used here is either the first line or a title that Auden added in later collections; some titles, noted here, have been supplied by the editor for this volume. Poems that Auden left unpublished, or that he printed in a magazine but did not collect in book form, are noted here.

It's No Use Raising a Shout (p. 3). Written November 1929.

What's in Your Mind, My Dove, My Coney (p. 5). Written November 1930.

Prothalamion (p. 6). Written Summer 1930 as a chorus for Auden's lost play *The Fronny;* used again in 1935 as a chorus in Auden and Christopher Isherwood's play *The Dog Beneath the Skin.*

Alma Mater (p. 8). Originally written in 1930 as a chorus for a nightclub scene in *The Fronny* and used again in 1933 as a chorus in Auden's play *The Dance of Death;* title supplied for this edition. Not published separately by Auden.

The Airman's Alphabet (p. 10). Written as a separate poem in June 1931 and shortly afterward incorporated into "Journal of an Airman" in *The Orators;* not published separately by Auden.

The Three Companions (p. 13). Written October 1931; originally the epilogue to *The Orators.*

Shorts (p. 14). Written 1929–1931; title supplied for this edition. Mostly unpublished during Auden's lifetime; some are printed here for the first time. "Let us honour if we can" (p. 15) was the dedicatory poem to Christopher Isherwood in Auden's first published volume, 1930 *Poems.* "Private faces in public places" (p. 16) was the dedicatory poem to Stephen Spender in *The Orators.* Auden and Isherwood used "If yer wants to see me agyne" (p. 17) and

"Alice is gone and I'm alone" (without the final stanza; p. 17) as songs in *The Dog Beneath the Skin*.

Song: You were a great Cunarder, I (p. 18). Written probably in 1932 and used as a song in *The Dance of Death;* not published separately by Auden.

Ballad: O what is that sound which so thrills the ear (p. 19). Written October 1932.

The Witnesses (p. 21). This is the complete version of this poem, written late in 1932 and, after appearing in *The Listener,* 12 July 1933, never reprinted or collected by Auden; he revised the third part as a chorus for *The Dog Beneath the Skin* and as a separate poem in later collections.

Song: Seen when night was silent (p. 27). Probably written in 1933; used as a song in *The Dog Beneath the Skin*.

Who's Who (p. 28). Probably written in 1934, after Auden reviewed a biography of Lawrence of Arabia.

Now Through Night's Caressing Grip (p. 29). Written 1935 as a chorus for *The Dog Beneath the Skin*.

In the Square (p. 30). Written Spring 1935; the title is from the poem's first appearance in *The Spectator,* 31 May 1935.

Madrigal (p. 32). Written June 1935 as a chorus, set by Benjamin Britten, for the documentary film *Coal Face,* made by the General Post Office Film Unit.

Night Mail (p. 33). Written July 1935 as a spoken commentary to the last part of the documentary film of the same name.

Song: Let the florid music praise (p. 36). Written February 1936.

Foxtrot from a Play (p. 37). Written March 1936; a few lines were used almost immediately as a song in Auden and Isherwood's play *The Ascent of F6.* The full text appeared under this title in *New Verse,* April–May 1936, but it was never collected by Auden.

Underneath the Abject Willow (p. 39). Written March 1936.

Fish in the Unruffled Lakes (p. 40). Written March 1936.

Song: The chimney sweepers (p. 41). Written probably in March 1936 for *The Ascent of F6,* but not published separately by Auden; title supplied for this edition.

At Last the Secret Is Out (p. 42). Written probably in April 1936 as a chorus for *The Ascent of F6*.

Funeral Blues (p. 43). First written in April 1936 for *The Ascent of F6;* rewritten in June 1937 as a cabaret song to be sung by Hedli Anderson. The version in *The Ascent of F6* was a dirge sung after the mountaineer hero dreams that his brother, a high colonial official, has suddenly died. In the play, the first two stanzas were the same as those in the rewritten version, but they were followed by these three stanzas, which refer to other characters who accompany the hero on his climb:

> Hold up your umbrellas to keep off the rain
> From Doctor Williams while he opens a vein;
> Life, he pronounces, it is finally extinct.
> Sergeant, arrest that man who said he winked!
>
> Shawcross will say a few words sad and kind
> To the weeping crowds about the Master-Mind,
> While Lamp with a powerful microscope
> Searches their faces for a sign of hope.
>
> And Gunn, of course, will drive the motor-hearse:
> None could drive it better, most would drive it worse.
> He'll open up the throttle to its fullest power
> And drive him to the grave at ninety miles an hour.

Jam Tart (p. 44). Written probably around April 1936 as a cabaret song to be set by Benjamin Britten and sung by Hedli Anderson; the title may have been chosen by Britten. First published posthumously in "Uncollected Songs and Lighter Poems, 1936–40," ed. by Nicholas Jenkins, *Auden Studies 2* (1994).

Death's Echo (p. 45). Written September 1936.

Letter to Lord Byron (p. 47). Written probably from July through October 1936.

Lullaby: Lay your sleeping head, my love (p. 86). Written January 1937.

Danse Macabre (p. 88). Written January 1937.

Blues: Ladies and gentlemen, sitting here (p. 91). Written probably early in 1937; printed in *New Verse*, May 1937, but never collected by Auden.

Give Up Love (p. 92). Written probably around April 1937 as a cabaret song to be set by Benjamin Britten and sung by Hedli Anderson; title supplied for this edition. First published posthumously in "Uncollected Songs and Lighter Poems, 1936–40," ed. by Nicholas Jenkins, *Auden Studies 2* (1994).

Nonsense Song (p. 94). Written probably in Spring 1937, perhaps for an anthology of children's poetry that was never published; title supplied for this edition. First published posthumously in "Uncollected Songs and Lighter Poems, 1936–40," ed. by Nicholas Jenkins, *Auden Studies 2* (1994).

Johnny (p. 95). Written April 1937.

Miss Gee (p. 96). Written April 1937.

Victor (p. 100). Written June 1937.

James Honeyman (p. 105). Written August 1937.

Roman Wall Blues (p. 110). Written October 1937 for the radio script *Hadrian's Wall*.

As I Walked Out One Evening (p. 111). Written November 1937.

O Tell Me the Truth About Love (p. 113). Written January 1938.

Gare du Midi (p. 115). Written in Brussels, December 1938.

Epitaph on a Tyrant (p. 116). Written January 1939.

The Unknown Citizen (p. 117). Written March 1939.

Refugee Blues (p. 118). Written March 1939.

Ode (p. 120). Written probably in March 1939; not published in Auden's lifetime. Auden inscribed the poem to the manager and staff of the hotel where he stayed during his first weeks in New York. S.A. = sex appeal.

Calypso (p. 122). Written May 1939.

Heavy Date (p. 123). Written October 1939.

Song: Warm are the still and lucky miles (p. 128). Written October 1939.

"Gold in the North" Came the Blizzard to Say (p. 129). Written probably around November 1939 for the libretto of the operetta *Paul Bunyan*.

The Glamour Boys and Girls Have Grievances Too (p. 130). Written probably around November 1939 for *Paul Bunyan;* published under this title in *The New Yorker,* 24 August 1940, but never collected by Auden.

Carry Her Over the Water (p. 132). Written probably in December 1939 for *Paul Bunyan.*

Eyes Look into the Well (p. 133). Written probably in April 1940 for the radio play *The Dark Valley.*

Lady Weeping at the Crossroads (p. 134). Written probably in April 1940 for *The Dark Valley.*

Notes (p. 136). Written Summer 1940 for the "Notes" to the long poem "New Year Letter."

The Way (p. 141). Written Summer 1940 as part of the sonnet sequence "The Quest."

Song for St Cecilia's Day (p. 142). Written July 1940.

Many Happy Returns (p. 145). Written February 1942.

Shepherd's Carol (p. 149). Written Spring 1942 for the long poem "For the Time Being: A Christmas Oratorio," but dropped before publication. Partly set by Benjamin Britten, who devised the title and published his setting. The full text is printed here for the first time. *Pinkie,* the standard children's word in America for the little finger, is virtually unknown in Britain.

Song of the Old Soldier (p. 151). Written Spring 1942 for "For the Time Being."

Song of the Master and the Boatswain (p. 152). Written around December 1942 for "The Sea and the Mirror: A Commentary on Shakespeare's *The Tempest.*"

Adrian and Francisco's Song (p. 153). Written around January 1943 for "The Sea and the Mirror." This early draft version is printed here for the first time; the version published in "The Sea and the Mirror" consists only of the third and second lines from the end.

Miranda's Song (p. 154). Written around January 1943 for "The Sea and the Mirror."

Three Songs from The Age of Anxiety (p. 155). Written probably in 1945 and 1946. In the prose narration in *The Age of Anxiety,* the first of these is described as a jukebox song titled "The Case is Closed" and the second is "a verse from an old prospector's ballad" (most of the suggestive terms have a technical use in mining). In the third song the four elements are identified indirectly: the "lake of hawks" is air; "sky of skulls" is earth; "melter of men and salt" is fire; "drinker of iron" is water.

Under Which Lyre (p. 157). Written Spring 1946 for the annual Phi Beta Kappa ceremony at Harvard University.

Nursery Rhyme (p. 163). Written January 1947.

Barcarolle (p. 164). Written around February 1948 for the libretto for *The Rake's Progress;* Auden collected the poem under this title in *The Shield of Achilles.*

Music Ho (p. 165). Written May 1948.

The Love Feast (p. 166). Written May 1948.

Song: Deftly, admiral, cast your fly (p. 167). Written June 1948.

Limericks (p. 168). Written Autumn 1950. Auden published three: "A Young Person," "T. S. Eliot," and "To get the Last Poems." The rest are here printed or collected for the first time, in texts found in Auden's letters to friends or, in the case of "Said the Queen to the King," transcribed from memory by Auden's friend Alan Ansen.

Hunting Season (p. 170). Written 1952.

The Willow-Wren and the Stare (p. 171). Written 1953.

The Proof (p. 173). Written August 1953.

"The Truest Poetry Is the Most Feigning" (p. 174). Written around September 1953.

Nocturne (p. 177). Written October 1953.

Metalogue to The Magic Flute (p. 178). Written 1955.

A Toast (p. 182). Probably written 1958, although not read at Christ Church, Oxford, until 1960.

Some Thirty Inches from My Nose (p. 184). Written around 1962.

On the Circuit (p. 185). Written around June 1963.

Song of the Ogres (p. 188). Written around December 1963 as one of the lyrics Auden was commissioned to write for the musical play *Man of La Mancha* before the producer turned to another lyricist.

Song of the Devil (p. 189). Written around December 1963 for *Man of La Mancha.*

The Geography of the House (p. 191). Written July 1964.

Moralities (p. 194). Written 1967.

A New Year Greeting (p. 201). Written May 1969.

Doggerel by a Senior Citizen (p. 203). Written May 1969.

Index of Titles and First Lines

A friend, who is not an ascetic, 168
A nondescript express in from the South, 115
A shilling life will give you all the facts, 28
A shot: from crag to crag, 170
A starling and a willow-wren, 171
A Young Person came out of the mists, 168
ACE—Pride of parents, 10
Adrian and Francisco's Song, 153
After vainly invoking the Muse, 168
Airman's Alphabet, The, 10
Alice is gone and I'm alone, 17
Alma Mater, 8
Among pelagian travelers, 185
Ares at last has quit the field, 157
As I Walked Out One Evening, 111
At Dirty Dick's and Sloppy Joe's, 152
At Last the Secret Is Out, 42
Ballad (O what is that sound which so thrills the ear), 19
Barcarolle, 164
Base words are uttered only by the base, 138
Blues (Ladies and gentlemen, sitting here), 91
By all means sing of love but, if you do, 174
Calypso, 122
Carry Her Over the Water, 132
Cleopatra, Anthony, 92
Come kiss me now, you old brown cow, 16
Danse Macabre, 88
Death's Echo, 45
Deep in my dark the dream shines, 155
Deftly, admiral, cast your fly, 167
Desire for death in the morning, 15
Do we want to return to the womb? Not at all, 137
Doggerel by a Senior Citizen, 203

Don't know my father's name, 16
—"Don't you dream of a world, a society with no coercion?", 140
Driver drive faster and make a good run, 122
Epitaph on a Tyrant, 116
Ever since observation taught me temptation, 189
Excuse, my lord, the liberty I take, 47
Eyes Look into the Well, 133
Fish in the Unruffled Lakes, 40
Foxtrot from a Play, 37
Fresh addenda are published every day, 141
Funeral Blues, 43
Gare du Midi, 115
Gently, little boat, 164
Geography of the House, The, 191
Give Up Love, 92
Glamour Boys and Girls Have Grievances Too, The, 130
"Gold in the North" Came the Blizzard to Say, 129
Hail the strange electric writing, 8
Hans-in-Kelder, Hans-in-Kelder, 139
He was found by the Bureau of Statistics to be, 117
Heavy Date, 123
His ageing nature is the same, 136
Hunting Season, 170
Hushed is the lake of hawks, 156
I am beginning to lose patience, 15
If yer wants to see me agyne, 17
In a garden shady this holy lady, 142
In an upper room at midnight, 166
In the First Age the frogs dwelt, 194
In the Square, 30
In this epoch of high-pressure selling, 120
Infants in their mothers' arms, 137
It's farewell to the drawing-room's civilised cry, 88
It's No Use Raising a Shout, 3
I'm a jam tart, I'm a bargain basement, 44
I'm afraid there's many a spectacled sod, 16
Jam Tart, 44
James Honeyman, 105
James Honeyman was a silent child, 105

Johnny, 95
Johnny, since today is, 145
Ladies and gentlemen, sitting here, 91
Lady Weeping at the Crossroads, 134
Lay your sleeping head, my love, 86
Let me tell you a little story, 96
Let the florid music praise, 36
Let us honour if we can, 15
Letter to Lord Byron, 47
Limericks, 168
Little fellow, you're amusing, 188
Love Feast, The, 166
Lullaby (Lay your sleeping head, my love), 86
Madrigal, 32
Make this night loveable, 177
Man would be happy, loving and sage, 14
Many Happy Returns, 145
Metalogue to The Magic Flute, 178
Miranda's Song, 154
Miss Gee, 96
Moralities, 194
Music Ho, 165
My Dear One is mine as mirrors are lonely, 154
My love is like a red red rose, 94
New Year Greeting, A, 201
Night Mail, 33
Nocturne, 177
Nonsense Song, 94
Notes, 136
Now Through Night's Caressing Grip, 29
Nursery Rhyme, 163
O for doors to be open and an invite with gilded edges, 30
O lift your little pinkie, 149
O lurcher-loving collier, black as night, 32
O Tell Me the Truth About Love, 113
O the valley in the summer where I and my John, 95
O what is that sound which so thrills the ear, 19
"O where are you going?" said reader to rider, 13
"O who can ever gaze his fill," 45

Ode, 120

On the Circuit, 185

On this day tradition allots, 201

Once for candy cook had stolen, 138

Only God can tell the saintly from the suburban, 140

Our earth in 1969, 203

Over the heather the wet wind blows, 110

Parents once upon a time, 136

Perfection, of a kind, was what he was after, 116

Pick a quarrel, go to war, 14

Private faces in public places, 16

Proof, The, 173

Prothalamion, 6

Refugee Blues, 118

Relax, Maestro, put your baton down, 178

Roman Wall Blues, 110

Said the Queen to the King: "I don't frown on", 168

Say this city has ten million souls, 118

Schoolboy, making lonely maps, 15

Seated after breakfast, 191

Seen when night was silent, 27

Sharp and silent in the, 123

Shepherd's Carol, 149

Shorts, 14

Some say that Love's a little boy, 113

Some Thirty Inches from My Nose, 184

Song (You were a great Cunarder, I), 18

Song (Seen when night was silent), 27

Song (Let the florid music praise), 36

Song (The chimney sweepers), 41

Song (Warm are the still and lucky miles), 128

Song (Deftly, admiral, cast your fly), 167

Song for St Cecilia's Day, 142

Song of the Devil, 189

Song of the Master and Boatswain, 152

Song of the Ogres, 188

Song of the Old Soldier, 151

Stop all the clocks, cut off the telephone, 43

T. S. Eliot is quite at a loss, 169

The Bishop-Elect of Hong Kong, 169
The Champion smiles—What Personality!, 138
The chimney sweepers, 41
The Emperor's favorite concubine, 165
The friends of the born nurse, 14
The lovely lawns are swarming, 153
The pleasures of the English nation, 15
The soldier loves his rifle, 37
"The Truest Poetry Is the Most Feigning", 174
Their learned kings bent down to chat with frogs, 163
There are two kinds of friendship even in babes, 16
There was a young poet whose sex, 169
These public men who seem so to enjoy their dominion, 139
This is the Night Mail crossing the Border, 33
Three Companions, The, 13
Three Songs from The Age of Anxiety, 155
To get the Last Poems of Yeats, 169
To the man-in-the-street, who, I'm sorry to say, 140
Toast, A, 182
Tommy did as mother told him, 14
Under Which Lyre, 157
Underneath the Abject Willow, 39
Unknown Citizen, The, 117
Victor, 100
Victor was a little baby, 100
Warm are the still and lucky miles, 128
Way, The, 141
What on earth does one say at a Gaudy, 182
What will cure the nation's ill?, 140
What's in Your Mind, My Dove, My Coney, 5
When Laura lay on her ledger side, 155
"When rites and melodies begin", 173
When statesmen gravely say—"We must be realistic—", 139
When the Sex War ended with the slaughter of the Grandmothers, 151
Who's Who, 28
Willow-Wren and the Stare, The, 171
Willy, finding half a soul, 15
With what conviction the young man spoke, 139
Witnesses, The, 21

You dowagers with Roman noses, 21
You were a great Cunarder, I, 18
You who return to-night to a narrow bed, 6
You're a long way off from becoming a saint, 14
You've no idea how dull it is, 130

About the Author

Wystan Hugh Auden was born in York, England, on February 21, 1907. He studied at Gresham's School, Holt, and Christ Church, Oxford, after which he lived for a year in a Berlin slum. In the early nineteen-thirties he taught school at Helensburgh, in Scotland, and then at the Downs School, near Malvern. In the later thirties he worked as a free-lance writer, and published travel books on Iceland (with Louis MacNeice) and the Sino-Japanese War (with Christopher Isherwood). Also in collaboration with Isherwood, he wrote three plays for the Group Theatre, London: *The Dog Beneath the Skin, The Ascent of F6,* and *On the Frontier.* In 1939 he left England for the United States, where he became a citizen in 1946. In America he lived in New York until 1941, then taught at Michigan and Swarthmore. In 1945 he served in Germany with the U.S. Strategic Bombing Survey, and, when he returned, again took an apartment in New York. From 1948 to 1972 he spent his winters in America and his summers in Europe, first in Ischia, then, from 1958, in a house he owned in Kirchstetten, Austria. During this period he wrote four opera libretti with Chester Kallman: *The Rake's Progress* (for Igor Stravinsky), *Elegy for Young Lovers* and *The Bassarids* (both for Hans Werner Henze), and *Love's Labour's Lost* (for Nicolas Nabokov). From 1956 to 1960 he spent a few months of each year in Oxford as the elected Professor of Poetry. In 1972 he left his winter home in New York to return to Oxford. He died in Vienna on September 29, 1973.

Edward Mendelson, the editor of this volume, is the literary executor of the Estate of W. H. Auden.

THE DYER'S HAND

In this volume, W. H. Auden assembled, edited, and arranged the best of his prose writings, including the famous lectures he delivered as Oxford Professor of Poetry. The result is a magnificent series of linked observations on poetry, art, and the observation of life in general. Surprisingly personal, this vastly erudite collection provides an intimate view of the author's mind, whose central focus is poetry, but whose province is the author's whole experience of the twentieth century.

Nonfiction/Literature/0-679-72484-2

FOREWORDS AND AFTERWORDS

Forewords and Afterwords reveals the same wit and intelligence—as well as the vision—that sparked the brilliance of Auden's poetry. The prose pieces in this collection highlight works by or about Alexander Pope, Vincent van Gogh, Thomas Mann, Virginia Woolf, Oscar Wilde, and A. E. Housman, or serve as introductions to editions of the classical Greek writers, the Protestant mystics, Shakespeare, Goethe, Kierkegaard, Tennyson, Grimm and Anderson, Poe, G. K. Chesterton, Paul Valéry, and others.

Nonfiction/Literature/0-679-72485-0